The
Exit Strategy
Handbook

The BEST Guide for a Business Transition

The EXIT STRATEGY HANDBOOK

Library of Congress Cataloging-in-Publication Data
is available upon request.

ISBN: 978-0-9886932-4-1

First Edition, April 2013
Fourth Edition, July 2016

CONTENTS

INTRODUCTION

The Exit Strategy Handbook is unique.

It is written for a unique audience that is about to go through a unique period of time.

This book is for owners of closely-held companies who want to sell their businesses in the next few years. You are unique because you represent only about 8% of the population in the United States, yet you employ between 60% and 70% of all US employees.

Most of your assets are found in the companies you own. The biggest anticipated check in your future is an eventual sale of your company to someone else, whether a third party, an ESOP, management or some other type of buyer. Your hope and dream is that someone will see the value in your company and pay the amount that you desire.

You are about to go through a unique period of time — something that has never happened in the history of mankind. There are about 78 million Baby Boomers who will retire in the next few years. These baby boomers own more than 4 million businesses, most of whom will try to sell their businesses to third parties during the next few years. This will create an unprecedented number of companies that will be available on the open market.

These companies will most likely be in competition with yours when you are ready to sell. We anticipate a buyer's market during the next few years, which will cause certain sellers to either not be able to sell their business or will sell the business for a lower-than-expected amount. Additionally, it is anticipated that income taxes and other taxes will increase in the near future, which might have the effect of possible reductions in obtaining values you might expect from the sale of your company.

The subtitle to this book is ***The Best Guide for a Business Transition***. This means that this book and the accompanying secured dashboard website have been prepared in a step-by-step process to help you sell your business. This process is similar to following the blueprint for a house or building. You are in charge of the blueprint, and you will delegate to people the tasks that will help you with the future desired sale of your business.

Survey at the Inc. 500|5000 Conference and Awards Ceremony

A business survey was conducted by B2B Exit®, a division of B2B CFO®, at the 2013 Inc. 500|5000 Conference and Awards Ceremony in Washington, D.C., held from Oct. 10-12, 2013. The surveyed business owners confidentially answered the following questions:

1. Are you a business owner?
2. Are you an Inc. 500 honoree, Inc. 5000 honoree or another business owner?
3. When would you like to sell your business?
4. What are your plans after you sell your business?
5. What are your concerns about selling your business?

When would you like to sell your business?

The following graph shows the responses of the 271 surveyed business owners:

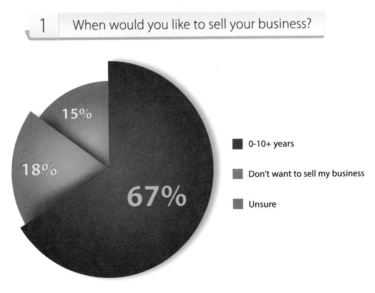

These 271 business owners consisted of the following types:

Inc. 500 honorees	21%
Inc. 5000 honorees	64%
Other owners	15%

Of these owners, 37% want to sell their business within 0 to 5 years, 20% want to sell between 6 and 10 years, and 10% desire the event to happen more than 10 years in the future. Of the respondents, 15% were unsure of when they want to sell their business, and about 18% do not want to sell their business.

What are your plans after you sell your business?

Business owners responded as follows regarding their plans after the sale of their business:

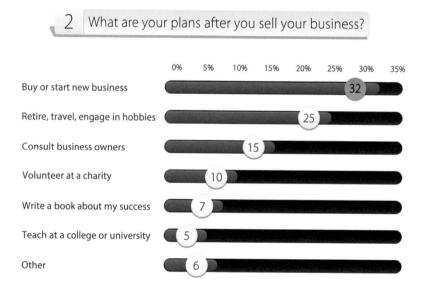

This survey indicates that 32% of the respondents are "serial business owners" who want to buy or start a new business after they sell their current business.

Only 25% of the owners want to retire, travel or engage in hobbies.

Approximately 27% of these owners want to pass their experiences to others by consulting for business owners, writing a book about their success, and teaching at a college or university.

Nearly 10% of them want to volunteer at a charity after the sale of their business.

More than 4% responded "other" regarding their plans following the sale of their business. It is not surprising that the answers varied. Some business owners said it is too early to sell their business, while others said they would stay on in their business.

There were those who said that after a sale they would start a foundation or run a non-profit organization. Then there were those business owners who said they were "not sure."

The more adventurous of the business owners said they wanted to learn how to fly.

There were also business owners who said they would like to combine the following: help other businesses grow, take time for themselves and give back to the community. Some even said they would choose all with the exception of charity work.

What are your concerns about selling your business?

Business owners responded as follows regarding their concerns about selling their business:

3   What are your concerns about selling your business?

- Valuation issues
- Sales price or net cash issues
- Owner or management issues
- Need help with the process
- Other

13%   11%   9%   18%   49%

Interestingly, almost half of business owners were concerned about the value of their company. Of these owners, 31% were not sure if the value of their company was high enough. Those with the highest concern about the value of their company were the Inc. 5000 winners, comprising almost 36% of total respondents.

Some of the most surprising responses to this survey were the almost 18% of business owners who did not know the value of their company. Of these owners, 80% were Inc. 500|5000 honorees. These owners represent some of the fastest-growing companies in America. They know the sales growth of their companies but not the correlation of the growth to the value of their companies.

Almost 11% had issues with management and conflicts with other business owners. There were 7% who admitted that they lacked a management team sufficient to sell their business. Almost 4% of the owners said they have conflicts with other owners within their business.

Almost 13% of these high achievers were uncertain about cash issues related to the sale, with almost 7% not knowing the amount of net cash needed from the transaction, and 6% did not know what price to charge for the sale of their company. Both of these issues may relate to lack of information regarding the correct market value of their company, which was a concern of almost 50% of the owners who took this survey.

About 10% of the owners had issues with time and assistance regarding the sale of their company. Almost 6% said they do not have time to start the process to sell their business, and about 4% said they need help to start the sales process.

While there are business owners who think about selling their business, they often have concerns about a sale. There are various reasons for not wanting to sell. When asked about the No. 1 concern about selling their business, almost 18% of owners' answers included being too young to sell, best timing, cannot decide on selling, the economy, and future work for family members.

One owner said his business may have garnered the attraction of one of the major ice cream brands to the point of a possible acquisition. Another owner said he would give the business to his family. Another owner expressed that growth opportunity is huge over the next five years.

Other answers included an owner who said, "I'm not replaceable enough," while some relayed that their business is a start-up. Another owner said, "It is so far out I would need someone else to plan." One said his businesses were just acquired, and another said, "Most M&A guys front private equity big guys who [do not care] about the owner really making money when they sell." Still another said, "Net proceeds after all selling cost." Included among the answers were some who said "none."

Additional answers from business owners included the following: not being in control, not ready, not ready yet, not really any concerns, not sure the company is marketable, not sure what to do next, pricing, selling too soon, starting, still having too much fun. One owner answered, "Taking care of the employees who believed in me and trusted me to do good by them." Still there were some owners who wrote timing, timing effect on leadership, timing...maturation, too many moving parts to the business model. Another answered, "Want to continue having fun and independence," while another said, "What to do after." Still another owner answered, "Wouldn't know what to do with myself."

Conclusion

Some important statistics from the survey findings include:

- 67% of surveyed business owners seek to sell their business within 10 years.
- 49% of surveyed business owners lacked knowledge of the market value of their business.
- Almost all the respondents had concerns, albeit varied, about how to sell their business.

Survey Details

When would you like to sell your business?

	Total		Inc. 500		Inc. 5000		Other Owners	
0-5 years	100	37%	22	40%	70	36%	8	20%
10+ years	26	10%	4	7%	15	7%	7	17%
6-10 years	53	20%	10	18%	36	19%	7	17%
I don't want to sell my business	50	18%	8	15%	32	23%	10	24%
Unsure	42	15%	12	20%	21	15%	9	22%
Grand Total	271	100%	56	100%	174	100%	41	100%

** Note: These numbers do not total 271 because some said they did not want to sell their business and others gave several answers to the question.

What are your plans after you sell your business?

	Total		Inc. 500		Inc. 5000		Other Owners	
Buy or start a new business	84	32%	18	32%	51	29%	15	52%
Retire, travel, engage in hobbies	65	25%	15	27%	44	25%	6	21%
Consult business owners	40	15%	9	16%	28	16%	3	10%
Volunteer at a charity	25	10%	5	9%	18	10%	2	7%
Write a book about my success	19	7%	4	7%	13	7%	2	7%
Teach at a college/university	12	5%	3	5%	9	5%	0	0%
Other	11	4%	0	0%	10	6%	1	3%
Help family members	7	2%	2	4%	5	2%	0	0%
Blank	0	0%	0	0%	0	0%	0	0%
Grand Total**	263	100%	56	100%	178	100%	29	100%

** Note: These numbers do not total 271 because some said they did not want to sell their business and others gave several answers to the question.

Survey Details (continued)

What are your concerns about selling your business?

	Total		Inc. 500		Inc. 5000		Other Owners	
Value not high enough	71	31%	11	24%	54	36%	6	21%
Don't know company's value	40	18%	6	13%	26	17%	8	28%
Other	40	18%	8	17%	24	16%	8	28%
Lack of a management team	16	7%	4	9%	11	7%	1	3%
Can't decide amount of net cash needed	15	7%	6	13%	8	5%	1	3%
Can't decide the sales price	14	6%	5	11%	7	5%	2	7%
No time to start the process	13	6%	3	7%	8	5%	2	7%
Conflicts with other owners	9	4%	1	2%	8	5%	0	0%
Need help starting process	9	3%	2	4%	6	4%	1	3%
Grand Total**	227	100%	46	100%	152	100%	29	100%

** Note: These numbers do not total 271 because some said they did not want to sell their business and others gave several answers to the question.

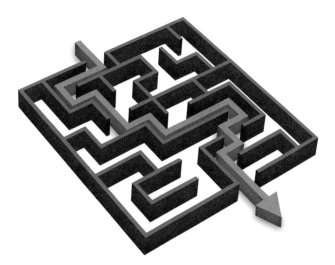

Chapter 1

Who Needs This Book?

The premise of this book is simple. It is a tool to help business owners sell their business.

There is no fluff or hyperbole in this book. It is results oriented with the goal of assisting business owners in solving a very complicated problem. *The Exit Strategy Handbook* is a process to help owners who:

	Attributes and Characteristics
1	Own a controlling interest in a closely-held (privately-owned) business
2	Want to sell the business during the next few years
3	Are proactive and willing to follow a step-by-step exit process
4	Either has or can have an Adjusted EBITDA of $1M or more

EXITING YOUR BUSINESS

Let's first be objective about your future exit from your current business. The following is from one of our books, Avoiding The Danger Zone, Business Illusions .[1]

> Benjamin Franklin is credited with the adage, "In this world nothing is certain but death and taxes." That statement is as true today as it was when he wrote it more than 200 years ago. We can add another truism for today's business owners: You will exit your company one day in the future.
>
> Your exit from your company may be planned or unplanned. The exit may bring satisfaction or dissatisfaction to you and your family. It may be to the benefit or detriment of your employees or associates. It may bring great financial reward, or it may bring financial devastation.
>
> The exit may bring fame or shame to your family and friends. It may be the continuance or discontinuance of the company you have worked so hard to build and create. The exit may be to the benefit or detriment of your competitors. Regardless of the consequences, you will someday exit your company in one form or another. [2]

THE BIG PICTURE

The beginning of the process to sell a business requires a certain mind-set. It requires a short-term focus. The beginning of the focus process is to accept that certain things are currently outside of your control, such as:

- The global economy
- The actions of leaders in Washington, D.C.
- The fair market value of assets that you own
- Future increases in income or estate taxes
- New regulations that might be imposed upon your business
- Etc.

It is natural to be concerned about such matters. Upon close examination, these are all long-term issues that are currently beyond your control.

The process of selling your business is a short-term project. You will have time and, hopefully, a lot of money to revert to being concerned about these subjects after the successful sale of your business.

The items above are a distraction and could impair your ability to focus on the goal of completing the sale of your business.

THE SHORT-TERM FOCUS

In the short-term, there are certain things that are under your control that require focus and attention, such as:

- Improving the value of your business
- Improving certain efficiencies within your business
- Associating with good exit strategy professionals
- Building a successful exit strategy team
- Following a step-by-step process to sell your business

The following, written by American theologian, Reinhold Niebuhr, might help us keep focused on the short-term things that are under our control.

> *God, give me grace to accept with serenity*
> *the things that cannot be changed,*
> *Courage to change the things*
> *which should be changed,*
> *and the Wisdom to distinguish*
> *the one from the other.* [3]

EXIT OPTIONS

We can look into your future and visualize the following exit options. One of these will occur to you:

- Work in the business until you die
- Semi-retire and let someone else run the business until you die
- Liquidate the assets of the business, either voluntarily or involuntarily
- Sell the business

We leave the first three of the above topics to other authors and professionals.

This book and its processes focus solely on the latter: **Sell the business**. Naturally, one of the concerns that business owners have is who will eventually buy their business.

POTENTIAL BUYERS

Business owners often have a lot of options related to this topic of selling a business. It is a myth that the sole option is to sell only to third parties.

There are multiple possible buyers for a closely-held business. Some of the most common possible buyers are:

- A strategic buyer
- A buyer who sees a financial opportunity
- Management Buyouts (MBO)
- Family members
- Employee Stock Ownership Plan (ESOP)
- Private Equity Groups (PEG)
- Initial Public Offering (IPO)
- Etc.

FINDING THE RIGHT BUYER

It is common for a business owner to become distracted about the potential buyer and what that buyer might do to the business long before there is even a discussion with the prospective buyer. Some of the most common concerns of business owners are:

- The legacy of the name and reputation of the business
- The price that will be paid
- The after-tax amount that will be available
- Whether the transaction will be paid in cash or in a long-term note
- Potential impacts of the sale to current employees
- Effects on family members working in the business
- Paying off the current debt owed by the business
- Disclosure of trade secrets before the transaction closes
- The length of time the owner will be required to stay after the sale
- Etc.

Our advice is not to be preoccupied with these issues at this time. There will be sufficient time to work on these details during our process. These burdens should be shifted off your shoulders and onto the shoulders of other people. We call these people *The Success Team™*.

THE SUCCESS TEAM™

One of the most important processes in this book is to surround yourself with *The Success Team™*, which is discussed in Chapter Three. It will be the job of the members of this team to help you find the right buyer for your business.

You will have adequate time and a proper format to tell the members of *The Success Team™* about your concerns. You will also be able to delegate to them the responsibility to help you with these important concerns. This team will help you with the exit plan.

THE EXIT PLAN

The exit plan will be created over a period of time using our process. An extremely successful entrepreneur said the following about not having an exit plan.

> *In the absence of a valid exit strategy, events will inexorably dictate the final exit plan for the business.*
>
> *Exit plans may be as varied as each venture's needs and purposes. In the absence of an Exit Plan, it is probable that an involuntary exit will be enforced by any number of circumstances: loss of market, competition, a better mouse trap, changes in customer acceptance, inept management, catering to wants instead of needs, lack of cost controls, etc.*
>
> *Gardner H. Russell* [4]

BEGIN WITH THE END IN MIND [5]

The late Stephen R. Covey was brilliant in this very simple concept of beginning with the end in mind. Regarding this subject, he stated:

> To begin with the end in mind means to start with a clear understanding of your destination. It means to know where you're going so that you better understand where you are now and so that the steps you take are always in the right direction.[6]

Dr. Covey not only emphasized going in the right direction, he also taught that it takes leadership to make sure one is going in the right direction. He taught the following about the difference between leadership and management:

Leadership is not management.

> *Management is doing things right; leadership is doing the right things.*

> *Management is efficiency in climbing the ladder of success; leadership determines whether the ladder is leaning against the right wall.*

> *The leader is the one who climbs the tallest tree, surveys the entire situation, and yells, "Wrong jungle."* [7]

THE RIGHT JUNGLE – THE FIRST DECISION

It is time to make the first important decision in this process.
The principles of this decision combine the teachings of Dr. Covey and Reinhold Niebuhr. This step is you taking the leadership to head in the right direction with the attitude of having courage to change those things that are within your power. The recommended decision is:

To increase the value of your business with the goal of having multiple bids to purchase your business.

In the short term, put behind the concern of who might someday buy your business. It is now time to begin the process to build so much value that, hopefully, you will have multiple buyers who might want to purchase your business.

DISTRACTIONS

This book will discuss that you will have competition from other sellers. They have no interest in your success. Their goal is to take away your buyer. You will have a significant competitive advantage over these competitors if you can eliminate certain distractions that will present themselves to you in the near future. The following about distractions is from one of our books:

> *Gordon Segal is the founder and CEO of Crate and Barrel, which he and his wife founded in 1962. The Retail Marketing Association voted Mr. Segal Retailer of the Year in 1996. Mr. Segal made one of the most profound business statements, which was documented in INC. Magazine:*
>
> *Getting distracted is the biggest problem entrepreneurs' face.*

The authors of *The Millionaire Next Door* said the same thing in different words:

> *Efficiency is one of the most important components of wealth accumulation. Simply: People who become wealthy allocate their time, energy and money in ways consistent with enhancing their net worth.* [8]

The process begins with the next chapter, exploring whether the future will be a buyer's or a seller's market for your company.

Chapter 2

The Future: A Buyer's or Seller's Market

An important part of the exit strategy process is to consider whether the eventual sale date of your business will occur during a buyer's or a seller's market. This will define whether you will be able to achieve the sales price you expect.

This topic will also be an important determination regarding the extent of the planning of the sale. Simply put, there are different strategic plans depending upon the projected existence of either a buyer's or a seller's market.

A SELLER'S MARKET

Some businesses are so unique or so superior to their competition that they will be able to command a seller's market, meaning they will have multiple buyers bidding for the purchase.

A BUYER'S MARKET

Many businesses are not viewed as unique. They have not put forth the effort to outclass their competition. These businesses run the risk of being viewed as a "commodity." The danger of being viewed as a commodity by the buyer community is the lack of distinguishing characteristics by the business that gives the potential buyer a significant advantage, which is to drive down the purchase price by competing one seller against the other. Under this scenario, the purchase price often goes to the lowest bidder. The risk in this situation is that you may not know how desperate the competition is to sell at a price much lower than the price you want or expect from the sale of your business. This scenario is the inverse of a seller's market.

A discussion about the future of either a buyer's or a seller's market is paramount for your company's future exit strategy success. Let's first discuss a seller's market.

TIMING FOR A BUYER'S OR A SELLER'S MARKET

Some businesses will leave the subject of selling during a buyer's or seller's market up to chance. They will be subject to certain business cycles. One expert made the following statement about a Ten-Year Transfer Cycle table:

> *Market timing is no less important than personal and business timing. There are opportunities to transfer a business in almost any type of economy. The unexpected knock on the door from an overpaying consolidator, however, happens only to the guy three lockers down. Everyone else must increase their market savvy to realize their goals. To maximize a transfer, a healthy transfer market is a good place to start. The U.S. transfer market seems to run in ten-year cycles, as shown in Exhibit 35.8.*

*Deal periods in a transfer cycle are not binary switches. Rather,
they are like leaky deal faucets. There are opportunities in every
period for an owner to create and maximize an exit. However,
sellers are most likely to get a good deal in a seller's market.*

Robert T. Slee [9]

United States Ten Year Private Transfer Cycle

Exhibit 35.8   Ten-Year Transfer Cycle

Reproduced with permission of John Wiley & Sons, Inc. Private Capital Markets, Valuation,
Capitalization, and Transfer of Private Business Interests, Second Edition, Robert T. Slee,©2011 by
Robert T. Slee, 565.

You should study whether you feel your business will sell during a buyer's
or seller's market.

You should also consider an unusual event that is about to occur that has
never happened in the history of mankind. First, we will propose an
analogy to introduce this most unusual upcoming event.

TSUNAMI

The Baby Boomer Tsunami™

© 2013 B2B CFO, LLC

We are familiar with the term "tsunami" mostly because of the devastation they cause when they hit land with large populations of people. For example, a tsunami in 2004 killed more than 230,000 people in 14 countries bordering the Indian Ocean.[10]

Tsunamis do not resemble tidal waves. They are often caused by earthquakes and can travel hundreds or even thousands of miles in a short period of time. A classic example happened on April 1, 1946. An earthquake with a 7.8 Richter Scale magnitude happened near the Aleutian Islands in Alaska. The earthquake created a tsunami, which headed south to Hawaii. The tsunami traveled more than 3,000 miles in 4.9 hours and hit Hilo on the island of Hawaii. One source recorded the waves as high as 46 feet and another states the waves were as high as a 13 story building. This tsunami caused 160 deaths.[11, 12]

One of the highest tsunamis happened in 1958 near Lituya Bay, Alaska. The tsunami reached a height of more than 1,700 feet. [13]
There is much that we do not know about tsunamis. There is one thing, however, that we can conclude. Once they begin their process and reach a certain height,

There is nothing we can do to stop them!

There is no wall that can quickly be constructed to stop the devastation. There is no equipment that can suddenly be moved into position to slow them down. They have a certain power and force of their own, and they will stop only when that force and power stops.

This phenomenon is analogous to an event with the Baby Boomer generation that might have a significant impact on whether your company will sell in a buyer's or a seller's market.

THE BABY BOOMERS

Now the Boomers are preparing to retire. They own more businesses than any generation before them, or probably than any in the future. The Baby Boomer business owners face a challenge like none other. Just as they have done everything else together, the Baby Boomer business owners are all going to sell their companies at the same time.

John F. Dini [14]

This kind of movement "could result in a glut of companies on the market, driving down valuations and giving new leverage to buyers."

John H. Brown [15]

The U.S. Census Bureau defines Baby Boomers as those born between Jan. 1, 1946, and Dec. 31, 1964. There are about 78,000,000 of them in the United States. They are beginning to retire. Assuming age 65 years old is the retirement age, they began to retire on Jan. 1, 2011. Assuming a straight-line retirement average, they will retire at a rate of about 4,105,000 a year through Dec. 31, 2029.

Let's relate this volume of Baby Boomers to future business exit strategies.

Bo Burlingham, author of Finish Big, wrote:

> According to a study by the U.S. Chamber of Commerce, just 20 percent of companies put up for sale are ultimately sold, meaning that four out of five prospective sellers walk away empty-handed. A much greater number of would-be sellers--by one estimate, 65 to 75 percent of owners who would like to sell--never even make it into the market. They learn early on that they have little or no chance of finding a buyer.
>
> The competition to cash out by selling to a PEG will only increase in the coming years, as **retiring baby boomers**--who by one estimate own **nearly four million** of the U.S. businesses that have employees--**flood the market**. [16]

One author predicts that 60% of U.S. businesses will transition to third parties:

> Today in the US, the majority of businesses are small businesses and most of them are family owned. Current statistics show that between 80 to 90% of businesses in the US are family owned.
>
> The average family business lasts 25 years; only 40% of the businesses go to the next generation.
>
> Frederick D. Lipman [17]

THE CHILDREN OF BABY BOOMERS

One can only speculate why only about 40% of businesses owned by Baby Boomers will be taken over by their children. One explanation may be that Baby Boomers gave birth to fewer children than did their parents.

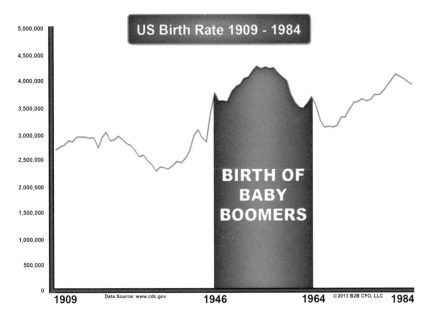

Another explanation could be that the children of Boomers left the family business at the requests, expectations and sacrifices of their parents. The Boomers wanted their children to go to college and become white-collar professionals, such as doctors, attorneys, dentists, orthodontists, bankers, accountants, educators, etc. Many of these children went into high-tech jobs when computers and technology exploded on the market.

Another motive may be that the children of Baby Boomers may have different interests and goals than their parents. They may not want to work as hard in a business created by their parents by working the number of hours their parents did in seemingly mundane and uninteresting tasks.

Regardless, they are moving on to other things and are letting about 60% of their family businesses either sell to others or liquidate.

IMPACT OF THE BABY BOOMERS

The above information is important in the analysis of the potential impact on the exit strategy of your business caused by the current retirement of Baby Boomers. Below is a recap and analysis of the above information:

1.   Retiring Baby Boomers will "***flood the market***."

2.   "*Baby Boomer business **owners are going to sell their companies at the same time**.*"

3.   This kind of a movement by Baby Boomers "***could result in a glut of companies on the market, driving down valuations and giving new leverage to buyers.***"

4.   Baby Boomers own about **4,000,000** U.S. businesses that have employees.

5.   Some kind of business transition must happen to these 4,000,000 companies because the Baby Boomers will someday, either retire or die.

6.   About **2,400,000** (60%) of these companies might be put on the market through either the end of the Baby Boomer retirement period or their death.

This information is important to know when compared to historical sales of privately-held companies.

Capital I.Q. (www.capitaliq.com) is a robust database that records mergers or acquisition transactions. This database shows the number of privately-held businesses that were acquired or merged during the past few years.

YEAR	NUMBER	CURRENT YEAR CHANGE
2009	5,835	-
2010	8,182	40%
2011	8,670	6%
2012	8,450	-3%
2013	8,339	-1%
2014	9,328	12%
2015	9,946	7%
2016	9,139	-8%
2017	15,755	72%
Average	9,294	

The average annual sales of privately-held businesses for the nine-year period listed above is 9,294. Let's be conservative and round that number to 10,000. That means that, based upon historical averages, about 200,000 privately-held companies will be sold during the next 20 years.

HISTORICAL SALES COMPARED TO FUTURE BABY BOOMER SALES

This 200,000 number is before the impact of the Baby Boomers, who might add **2,400,000** companies on the market during the next 20 years.

We learned earlier in this chapter that a majority of privately-held businesses that want to go to market will never make it. This may not, however, keep the Baby Boomers from trying to sell their companies. Some may be desperate enough to significantly lower the sales price of the business in order to get something for all of the decades of their hard work. The impact of the volume of potential sales is staggering, as is shown on the next page.

HISTORICAL SALES COMPARED TO FUTURE
BABY BOOMER SALES

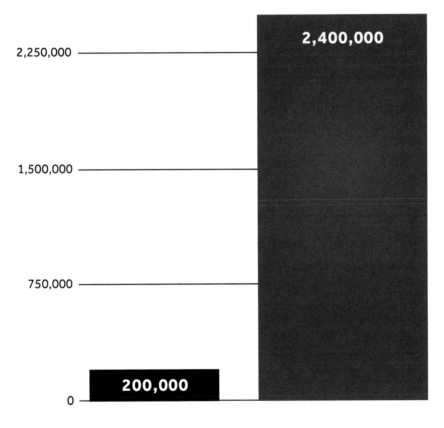

2,250,000

2,400,000

1,500,000

750,000

200,000

0

■ Projected sales based upon historical numbers

■ Baby Boomer companies, non-family transfers

THE BABY BOOMER TSUNAMI™

The sheer volume of Baby Boomers who will put companies on the market is similar to the previous discussion above about a tsunami.

There is nothing we can do to stop them!

The Baby Boomers are going to put their companies on the market. Obviously, many of these companies will never be purchased. Many will simply liquidate their assets due to a lack of demand from buyers. Many hopes and dreams of successful exit strategies will be dashed. Many lives will be impacted by this occurrence.

The increased volume has the likelihood of creating a buyer's market for many companies.

A BUYER'S MARKET

What, if anything, can you do about this phenomenon of *The Baby Boomer Tsunami* ™ regarding your exit strategy process?

We propose that you explore this subject with a team of professionals we call *The Success Team*™, discussed in the next chapter.

Chapter 3
The Success Team™

Your first step should be to assemble an outstanding professional team to advise you. Most business people select their professional team on the eve of their sale. This is far too late in the sale process. By selecting your professional team several years before the target date for your sale, you can obtain their guidance in the presale years as to methods of minimizing the obstacles.

Frederick D. Lipman [18]

On the next page are the team members we recommend for *The Success Team*™ and a brief description of their roles during this process.

The Success Team™

Title	Role	Goal
Business Owners	Direction and final decisions	Increase sales and company value
B2B CFO®	Team Manager	Coordinate the Team, assist with process
M&A Company or Investment Banker	Advice about potential buyers	Find the best buyer
Attorney	Legal	Legal documentation and advice
Tax Specialists	Tax planning	Tax planning
Auditors	Auditing	Examine financial statements
IT Specialists	Software and hardware	Documentation and advice
Wealth Manager	Money management advice	Pre-sale advice and post-sale wealth management
Appraiser	Appraise the company	The business value and the primary methods of valuation
Insurance Advisor	Insurance advice	Advice on current and future risks
Banker	Lending advice	Assist with lending activities
Key Employees	Support	Information and transition
Directors, Executive Coaching Organizations, etc.	Advisory	Advice and consultation

BUSINESS OWNERS
(Finder)

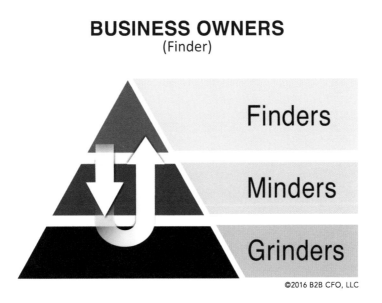

Finders

Minders

Grinders

©2016 B2B CFO, LLC

The business owner is usually the Finder in the business. This is the most important role on *The Success Team*™ during the exit strategy process. The business owner is the Finder and the principal roles in the company are to be:

> *The entrepreneur, the visionary, the leader, the idea generator and the catalyst for future change. Finders work in the future.* [19]

This is your business. You are in charge. Your most effective role on *The Success Team*™ is to:

- Select outstanding professionals.
- Delegate key tasks to these team members.
- Use our process to track their progress.
- Spend most of your time in Finding activities.

Many business owners get distracted during the exit strategy process and find themselves involved in performing administrative tasks (Minding). This is a serious mistake. The business owner should continue to increase the value of the business. This is typically done by continued focus on those things that increase the future value of the business. Those activities are typically increasing sales, finding new customers, building better relationships with current customers, etc.

BUSINESS OWNERS
INCREASED VALUE THROUGH EBITDA

We will spend time on topics such as earnings before interest, taxes, depreciation and amortization (EBITDA) later in this book, which can be a key method to determining the value of your business. An author has stated the following about increasing EBITDA during the exit strategy process:

> For each $1 that you increase your EBITDA during the valuation year, you should arguably receive an additional $4 to $6 in sale price.
>
> Frederick H. Lipman [20]

Mr. Lipman is suggesting that for each $1 million you increase EBITDA during the exit strategy process, you should see an additional $4 million to $6 million in sales price!

We propose that there is nobody on *The Success Team*™ who has your talent and drive to increase the future sales price to this degree. We recommend you delegate important tasks to others in *The Success Team*™ and keep your focus on increasing the value of the company. That is, after all, the best use of your talents.

TEAM MANAGER

Most exit strategy experts recommend hiring an outside person to lead *The Success Team*™.

> Retain a point person. Even with an inside sale, I believe a third party point person is essential.
>
> Rick Rickertsen [21]

There is no requirement that the Team Manager be an outside person. There are, however, some advantages to hiring an outside nonemployee as the Team Manager. This person:

- Has experience in the exit strategy process
- Is not worried about losing a W-2 job when the transaction closes
- Is focused solely on completing the exit strategy process

- Will help the other team members keep focused on their deadlines
- Can easily communicate important concerns and issues directly to you
- Allows you to spend less time delegating and following up on matters
- Will give you more time to focus on increasing the value of the business

We recommend the Team Manager use this book and the accompanying dashboard software to help manage *The Success Team*™.

M&A COMPANY OR INVESTMENT BANKER

The role of this team member is to find the right buyer for your business. As one author states:

> *They act as sage counsel, uncover a large universe of buyers, run your auction, take on the role of the bad guy so the business owner doesn't have to. They run great interference and know how to play buyers off against one another to get you the absolute best deal. And they normally can smoke out when a buyer is not real, which can save you huge amounts of time and money. Remember, their fees are nearly all success-based. They only get real money if you get real money.* [22]

These companies will ask you to sign a lengthy and binding contract. They will want exclusivity from their competition. This means you must carefully consider hiring the right company. The attorney on *The Success Team*™ should be involved in this process and should review all documents prior to signing.

ATTORNEY

The attorney hired to be on *The Success Team*™ should be experienced in exit strategy sales transactions. There will be many documents and much advice needed from this professional.

One of the key documents this attorney will create or review for you is the confidentiality and nondisclosure documents to be signed by the potential buyer. It is paramount that you not divulge trade secrets, key information about customers and other critical information until the attorney and other team members feel you have as much protection as possible in dealing with potential buyers.

In short, no document should be signed in the exit strategy process without the review, input and advice from the attorney on *The Success Team*™.

TAX SPECIALISTS

Tax specialists are tax attorneys and Certified Public Accountants (CPAs) who are specialists in taxes in the following areas:

- Federal income taxes
- State income taxes
- Foreign taxes
- Personal property taxes
- Real estate taxes
- Sales and use taxes
- Payroll and withholding taxes
- Estate taxes
- Etc.

The role of the tax expert is more than simply calculating the net cash available to you after the sales transaction. This professional's role is also to look for and advise you regarding any unrecorded or potential taxes that may possibly be a surprise to you prior or subsequent to the sale.

Taxation is usually a very frustrating part of the exit strategy process. Many business owners assume they will receive capital gains treatment on the sales proceeds. They frequently are surprised to know that there are often material items in the transaction that receive ordinary income treatment, such as the recapture of accumulated depreciation.

No purchase offer should be seriously considered until the tax specialists of *The Success Team*™ have had adequate time to thoroughly calculate and educate all members of the team on all potential tax issues that might occur prior or subsequent to the sales transaction.

AUDITORS

The buyer may require an examination by an independent CPA firm for two or three years prior to the sale. The buyer will rely on the examinations performed by the independent CPA firm to determine if the financial statements of your company have integrity.

> *The lack of financial integrity is one of the most common hurdles encountered during the sale process. In addition, the best way to demonstrate the sustainability of your company's earnings is to have its historical financial statements audited by an independent, certified public accounting firm. An audit demonstrates to the potential buyers that the historical information can be relied upon when making judgments about buying the company based on historical cash flows. It is very important to have your CPA review your current financial statements and practices so that any financial irregularities or inadequacies are immediately exposed and corrected.*
>
> *John H. Brown* [23]

One of the most difficult decisions you and *The Success Team*™ will have to make is whether you should hire your own auditors or allow the buyer to hire their own auditors. There are pros and cons to each of these decisions, which will be discussed in a subsequent chapter of this book.

IT SPECIALISTS

The IT specialist is a very important member of *The Success Team*™. This professional will advise the other team members regarding certain important information about the company, such as:

- Licensed or unlicensed software used by the company
- Software owned by the company
- URLs and websites owned by the company
- Restrictions of transfers or changes in control of software
- Ownership and location of important hardware
- Ownership, location and control of cloud-based software
- Passwords and usernames of all software used
- Etc.

The Success Team™ should work together to hire the best person or company possible to provide this function in the exit strategy process.

WEALTH MANAGER

Many business owners wait until the transaction closes before they talk to their wealth manager about their options to invest the net cash from the sales transaction. This delay in talking to the wealth manager could possibly be the largest mistake you could make during the exit strategy process.

> *(Baby) Boomers need a lot of money when we leave our companies because we will live longer than our parents did and we want to be active. Living longer and more actively means we need more money than we may have originally thought.*
>
> *What this means to you is that you'll likely have decades to live after you leave your company. The challenge is to create a nest egg big enough to (1) cover the expensive medical care, including even more life extending and quality of life treatments, (and if not that, the expensive health insurance premiums) we'll want and need as we age; and (2) last until we die.*
>
> *We Boomers have a lot of living left to do and we want to live well.*[24]

Wealth managers should be brought into *The Success Team*™ early in the process. These professionals need to work with the tax specialists and others on the team. They will need to know the estimated value of the assets that will be available after taxes to provide for your financial future. It is also important for them to hear if the auditors feel significant adjustments will be made that might impact the value of the sale. Additionally, they need to work with the M&A firm/Investment Bankers to understand what type of buyer will eventually purchase your company.

Wealth managers also need to know if the purchase price will be all cash or if there will be a note payable. Most importantly, these professionals need time with you to find out what your post-sale goals and needs will be in order to ensure that you will be able to accomplish those goals and needs from a financial perspective. Wealth managers will be very focused on your quality of life once the sale of your company has been completed. They will work with you and your future generations to preserve and grow the liquidity that is created by the sale both now and in the foreseeable future.

APPRAISER

Your company will want to receive a preliminary appraisal prior to bringing in a potential buyer. *The Success Team*™ will help advise you on the timing of this appraisal.

You can look at this process as similar to that of selling a home. Let's say you want to sell your home for a certain sales price. It makes sense to receive a preliminary appraisal before spending too much money on fixing up the home and putting it on the market.

> *An appraisal of your business, which specifies the primary valuation methods and factors, should be sought from a qualified appraiser well in advance of the expected sale date. Such an appraisal could cost as little as $5,000 to $10,000. Select the appraiser by reputation and personal recommendation.*
>
> *What is important is not so much an appraisal of what your business is currently worth but rather an understanding of the primary methods of valuation and valuation factors.* [25]

The timing of this appraisal should be decided by *The Success Team*™. The entire team could then use the assumptions and information used in the appraisal to determine a strategy to be used for the exit strategy process.

INSURANCE ADVISOR

The insurance advisor's role in the exit strategy process is to help *The Success Team*™ with certain documentation and planning.

The documentation will relate to the location and termination dates of certain important insurance policies, such as property and casualty, general liability, automobile, errors and omissions, directors and officers, key man life, disability, health, business interruption, bonds, umbrella, workers compensation, etc. It is important for the insurance advisor to advise *The Success Team*™ so that these and other important policies remain in effect during the exit strategy process and through the close of the sale transaction. The insurance advisor may recommend that some insurance policies remain in place after the close of the sale transaction.

An important role of the insurance advisor is to assist *The Success Team*™ in preparing for the unexpected events. The age-old adage applies with this professional, "Hope for the best and prepare for the worst." Numerous unplanned events may take place during the exit strategy process, and it is wise to be as prepared as possible for them:

- The untimely death of the business owner
- The untimely death of a minority business owner
- Unexpected claims on insurance policies
- Significant changes in insurance policies by insurance carriers
- Untimely termination of insurance policies by insurance carriers
- Accidents that are not adequately covered by existing insurance policies
- Etc.

The insurance advisor should be aware of the plans and activities of *The Success Team*™ to help them achieve their exit strategy goals.

BANKER

Bankers are seasoned business advisors. Many have seen their customers go through an exit strategy.

Nobody can predict the date when your company will be sold. The process may take a few months or a few years. Your company needs to continue its operations on a day-to-day basis, and bankers are an integral part of helping the company with its operational lending needs.

One of the key principles in this book is the concept of increasing sales to increase company value prior to the sale. Bankers understand that increases in sales often negatively affect the cash flow of the company. They realize that increased sales will cause increases in accounts receivable, inventory, fixed assets, overhead, etc., which often cause a decrease in cash.
Bankers should assist your company through this process to help with increases in lending of lines of credit and other loan instruments.

It is easier for bankers to know your company's lending and banking needs if they are a part of *The Success Team*™. This gives them the opportunity to understand the needs of the company and to possibly act quicker on creating loan instruments.

The business advice of these experienced veterans is often very valuable, and their input should be asked throughout the exit strategy process.

Bankers can also help fund some of the purchase. Your banker should be considered as a possible resource to assist with the funding of the transaction with the buyer.

KEY EMPLOYEES

Key employees can make or break the sale of your business. Some of them will become an important part of the process of assisting *The Success Team*™ and the transition subsequent to the close of the sale. These employees will eventually hear about your desire to sell your business. Some of their immediate concerns might be:

- The possible loss of their job and benefits
- Not working in the future with you
- Possible changes in the culture of the company
- The stress of working for another company, different management, etc.
- Changes in salary or benefits
- Job insecurity

The Success Team™ needs to advise you about how to deal with key employees before they are told about your desire to sell the business. One author provides the following advice:

> *Don't issue stock options to retain key employees after an acquisition. Instead, use a simple stay bonus that offers the member of your management team a cash reward if you sell your company. Pay the reward in two or more installments only to those who stay so that you ensure your key staff stays on through the transition.*

> *John Warrillow* [26]

The Success Team™ might consider advising you on matters such as the following:

- Cash bonuses
- The signing of confidentiality agreements
- The signing of long-term employment agreements
- Training of key employees about disclosures to other employees, vendors, customers, etc.

Dealing with key employees should be very high on the planning list of *The Success Team*™.

BOARD OF DIRECTORS, EXECUTIVE COACHING ORGANIZATIONS, ETC.

Some business owners have relationships with outside individuals and/or organizations. These might include a board of directors, an executive committee, an executive coaching organization, etc. The business owner might consider the expertise of these individuals and/or organizations when deciding whether to include them on *The Success Team*™ because they might have a very positive influence during the process.

Chapter 4

The Realistic Value of Your Business

You can increase the value of your business if you understand how buyers are likely to value it.

Frederick D. Lipman [27]

Any profitable business can be sold. It's just a matter of value, terms and structure. Total company value is not always equal to the cash received at the close of the sale of the business.

Larry Reinharz, Managing Director, Woodbridge International

This chapter will give you and *The Success Team*™ the tools to arrive at a realistic value of your business. These tools will also be able to be used to determine if the value of your business materially increases or decreases during the exit strategy process.

The subject of the realistic value of your business can be one of the most difficult topics during the exit strategy process. Business owners often feel:

- Buyers and appraisers are intentionally undervaluing the business
- The prospective buyer does not really understand the true value of the business

- The various valuation methods are not realistic ways to calculate value
- Not enough value is given to intangibles, such as employees, customers, etc.

DIFFERENT VALUATION METHODS

The process of placing a consistent dollar value on your business can be very frustrating. One of the frustrations is the numerous ways that buyers and appraisers use to value a business. Additional irritation arises because some appraisers use two or more valuation methods within the same report. Below are some of the most common valuation methods: [28]

- EBITDA Method
- Discounted Cash Flow Method
- Comparable Company Method of Valuation
- Comparable Transaction Method of Valuation
- Asset Accumulation Method
- Acquisition Debt Value
- Liquidation Value

The following is an example of how difficult this subject is and how different valuation methods can create significantly different results. In this fictitious example, the company name is PrivateCo, which is owned by Joe Mainstreet. The same financial information (Balance Sheet and Income Statement) was used to determine all of the following values.

EXHIBIT 3.5   PrivateCo Valuation by World

World	Value
Asset market value	$2.4 million
Collateral value	$2.5 million
Insurable value (buy/sell)	$6.5 million
Fair market value	$6.8 million
Investment value	$7.5 million
Impaired goodwill	$13.0 million
Financial market value	$13.7 million
Owner value	$15.8 million
Synergy market value	$16.6 million
Public value	$18.2 million

Reproduced with permission of John Wiley & Sons, Inc. Private Capital Markets, Valuation, Capitalization, and Transfer of Private Business Interests, Second Edition, Robert T. Slee,©2011 by Robert T. Slee, 49.

This author said the following about this table:

> If PrivateCo's owner Joe Mainstreet is advised that his company is worth a specific dollar value and that all of his decisions should revolve around that value, Joe and PrivateCo could suffer as a result of that advice.
>
> Robert T. Slee [29]

Let's imagine that Joe Mainstreet is advised to use the Public Value of $18.2M in his exit strategy planning. There are multiple decisions that Joe Mainstreet could make using this value, such as:

- Net cash available after paying ordinary and capital gains taxes
- Bonuses to be paid to key employees and management
- Company and personal debt to be paid
- Personal assets to be purchased after the close
- Investments to be managed by wealth managers after the close
- Commitments to various favorite charities
- Travel and other post-sale plans, etc.

Let's now imagine that the top buyer approaches Joe Mainstreet and offers the Fair Market Value ($6.8M), which is $11.4M less than he was expecting. It is highly likely that all of the decisions he made based on the $18.2M Public Value are wrong. Hence, Mr. Slee's statement is absolutely correct, "Joe and PrivateCo could suffer as a result of that advice."

YOUR COMPANY'S BALANCE SHEET

Your company's balance sheet has assets, tangible and intangible, that may have value to the future buyer. Those assets will be valued using certain methods sometime before the purchase. The process in this chapter will not calculate the value of those assets. Rather, their value will be deferred to the future until your company is closer to bringing in a potential buyer.

The buyer will determine which of your company's assets it wants to purchase. Be prepared for the buyer to not be interested in purchasing some of your company's assets, such as your building.

BALANCE SHEET ERRORS

It has been our experience that almost all companies have material errors on their balance sheets. These errors are often compounded if the company owns subsidiary companies. These errors may have a significant impact on the valuation process to be explained below. It is critical to fix any potential errors on the balance sheet prior to going through the valuation process explained in this chapter.

THE EBITDA METHOD

A number of businesses are valued by buyers based upon accounting earnings or income. Indeed, one of the most common methods of valuation is the so-called EBITDA method. This involves the determination of your accounting earnings before interest, taxes, depreciation, and amortization (EBITDA), and multiplication of the EBITDA by the relevant multiplier to obtain a business valuation.

Frederick D. Lipman [30]

The main indicator of value, to a PEG (Private Equity Group), or other buyer, is earnings before interest, taxes, depreciation and amortization, or EBITDA. EBITDA is a framework that allows buyers to compare "apples to apples" instead of "apples to oranges" when viewing businesses with different operating structures.

Robert W. Scarlata [31]

For each $1 that you increase your EBITDA during the valuation year, you should arguably receive an additional $4 to $6 in sale price.[32]

This chapter will illustrate several steps to the valuation of your company using the EBITDA method along with an explanation of these steps:

- The EBITDA calculation
- Adjustments to EBITDA
- EBITDA multipliers
- The format for the Adjusted EBITDA valuation
- EBITDA valuation periods

THE EBITDA CALCULATION

The calculations below assume two types of companies: taxable and pass-through. A taxable entity is a C-Corporation. Pass-through entities are typically S-Corporations, limited liability companies (LLC), partnerships or sole proprietorships.

DESCRIPTION	TAXABLE ENTITY	PASS-THROUGH ENTITY
Revenue	$9,000,000	$9,000,000
Cost of sales	6,000,000	6,000,000
Gross profit	3,000,000	3,000,000
Administrative expense	1,900,000	1,900,000
Income before taxes	1,100,000	1,100,000
Income taxes	440,000	--
Income after taxes	$660,000	$1,100,000
EBITDA calculation		
Income after taxes, above	$660,000	$1,100,000
Interest expense	180,000	180,000
Income taxes	440,000	--
Depreciation expense	105,000	105,000
Amortization expenses	15,000	15,000
EBITDA	$1,400,000	$1,400,000

ADJUSTMENTS TO EBITDA

The difficult part of using EBITDA as a valuation method is the identification of adjustments to EBITDA, which are usually items that might be considered distortions to the EBITDA calculation by prospective buyers. *The Success Team*™ needs to spend time identifying and discussing any possible adjustment to EBITDA long before an examination is performed by independent CPAs and before any discussion with prospective buyers.

Your EBITDA is then adjusted to remove expenses and revenue that will no longer be carried forward into the new business. These adjustments can be quite substantial for a closely held family business.

Most closely held businesses are operated to minimize income taxes. As a result, excessive compensation and perquisites may be provided to the owner and his family in order to reduce taxes. The excessive compensation and perquisites are really forms of disguised dividends.

Frederick D. Lipman [33]

One of the most frequent errors in performing this kind of analysis is to take the EBITDA or EBIT numbers at face value, without considering whether these numbers really reflect the true economic performance of your company.

Your financial statements will seldom reflect the real economic performance of your company. Numerous distortions may creep in.

Les Nemethy [34]

It is important to understand that *The Success Team*™ and a prospective buyer are not judging your business acumen on the decisions you have made on certain expenses in the Income Statement. Rather, they are trying to evaluate what the EBITDA of the company might be under normal circumstances. The prospective buyers are also trying to compare your company to similar types of companies in order to determine which company, if any, they might want to purchase. It is very important to be open with the members of *The Success Team*™ and to not take personal offense about this discussion. The goal of *The Success Team*™ is to help you through a most difficult process.

Some business owners face the issues of income tax avoidance and income tax evasion during this process. This topic will be covered in a subsequent chapter of this book.

As a way to illustrate this subject of adjustments to EBITDA, let's look at a potential adjustment that would be a decrease to EBITDA.

> *The owner/manager of Company A draws no salary from the company. His market salary would be $200,000 per year, or $250,000 grossed up with all payroll and social security taxes. If an investor were to buy this business, the former owner/manager would presumably not be prepared to stay and work for free indefinitely; nor would a replacement be willing to work for free. Presumably the new managers would ask for a market salary. Hence EBITDA and EBIT (Earnings before interest and taxes) would be diminished by $250,000.* [35]

This example makes sense. You would do the same if you were considering purchasing a company. You would look at the Income Statement to see if the owner/manager had not been deducting a salary. Your first reaction would be something like, "It will cost me at least $250,000 to replace this guy, so I am going to lower my offer to this company because of my future costs that are not currently recorded in this company's expenses."

Again, this is not a judgment of your business acumen. Rather, it is a prudent analysis by a prudent potential buyer about the future increase in operational costs of your business. This is merely a business decision that must be made by the prospective buyer. It is also a business analysis that should be considered by *The Success Team™*.

Below is an example of an adjustment that would be an increase to EBITDA.

> *The son of the owner/manager of Company B is 17 years old and is working part-time for Company B, drawing a salary of $100,000 (fully grossed up). The son is not producing anything of value for Company B, nor would the investor wish to continue with the son on the payroll. In this case, EBITDA and EBIT would be increased by $100,000.* [36]

Some owners can get a bit extravagant in their expenses to the company.

> *The owner of Company C purchased four helicopters. This was not at all necessary for operation of the company's core business (This has actually happened!). The $450,000 required for the operation of the helicopters should be added back to EBITDA and EBIT.* [37]

Some business owners can become very creative on the topic of writing off personal expense in the company's Income Statement:

> I know a businessman in Texas who writes off almost $10,000 annually on his personal "work boots." He really does purchase the boots, but they tend to come in exotic leathers like ostrich and boa constrictor, and he seldom wears them to work. [38]

Below is a list of potential discretionary items in the Income Statement that may be adjustments to EBITDA. These adjustments may be either increases or decreases to EBITDA and may have a material impact on the valuation of the business:

- Excessive compensation to owners, management and employees
- Personal legal costs for estate planning, divorce, personal litigation, etc.
- No income or below-market income to owners and management
- Tuition and educational expenses for children and family members
- Cash donations to charitable organizations
- Golf, country club or other such expenses not really necessary to the business
- Nepotism expenses (salary, autos, computers, vacations, etc.)
- Vacations or other related party travel expenses, including time-share expenses, etc.
- Multiple vehicles or unusual vehicle expenses for the owner, family, etc.
- Excessive insurance to owners and related parties (e.g., life, health, disability)
- Building rent paid to an owner that is in excess of or under market value
- Equipment leases paid to an owner that are in excess of or under market value
- Professional sports tickets not necessary for the business
- Rental expenses or repairs that would normally be paid by a landlord
- Hobbies such as buying jewelry, antique cars, etc.
- Below-market transfers of assets to related parties or family members
- Discounted sales prices to related parties, friends, etc.
- Costs paid in excess of market to vendors who are related parties or friends
- Discounts or free delivery given to related parties or friends

- Repairs, remodeling, maintenance, insurance or other expenses for a personal residence
- Inventory or scrap sold in cash and not deposited into the company's bank account
- Alimony or child-support payments made by the company
- Bonuses or other perks that are above-market costs, etc.

Not all adjustments are discretionary items such as the above examples. Some adjustments are one-time or otherwise unusual expenses.

> *My company negotiated the sale of a business that was operating a large fleet of trucks. Suddenly, fuel prices shot up to unprecedented levels. We assessed the situation and found reason to believe that fuel prices would be more stable in the future. In preparing the profit and loss statement for EBITDA purposes, we recast the most recent fuel costs to more reasonable levels.*
>
> *Robert W. Scarlata* [39]

Below are examples of one-time, nonrecurring or unusual expenses that might be included in adjusted EBITDA:

- Maintenance capital expenditures
- IT capital expenditures
- Write-off of an unproductive or obsolete asset
- Unusual, one-time or prior period adjustments proposed by independent CPAs
- Legal expenses incurred for the exit strategy
- Legal costs of restructuring or reorganization
- Audit, appraisal or consulting fees for the exit strategy
- Litigation expenses that have concluded and are nonrecurring
- Costs of exits of minority owners prior to the sale of the company
- Insurance claims
- Opening a new facility
- Writing off inventory that is unusual or nonrecurring
- Unusual bad-debt expenses, such as a Chapter 11 bankruptcy filing by a customer
- Employment costs, such as large severance or other nonrecurring expenses
- Large and unusual bonuses or other compensation paid for nonrecurring transactions

- Differences between book and tax depreciation
- Professional fees, such as creating a Defined Contribution or Benefit Plan
- Leases that were expensed instead of being capitalized
- Equipment that was expensed instead of being capitalized
- One-time marketing, branding, public relations or research costs

In short, *The Success Team*™ should carefully comb through the Costs of Sales, Selling, General and Administrative and Other Expense categories to determine if there are one-time, nonrecurring or unusual expenses in the Income Statement. As a rule of thumb: When in doubt, disclose the item and place it in adjusted EBITDA.

EBITDA MULTIPLIERS

Once adjusted, EBITDA needs to be multiplied by a certain range of numbers that are called "multipliers." These numbers are used to help with the estimated valuation of your business.

> *The adjusted EBITDA is then multiplied by a multiplier to obtain an overall valuation for the business (also called "enterprise value"). The multiplier typically ranges from 4 to 6 times adjusted EBITDA, particularly for financial buyers. However, the multiplier has gone below 4 and substantially above 6, depending upon whether it is a buyer's market or a seller's market for the sale of businesses. A multiplier above 6 is more typical for strategic rather than financial buyers.*

> *Multipliers of 20 or more are not unheard of for strategic buyers of companies with strong market niches.*

> *The multipliers are derived from comparable company valuations, including the multipliers applicable to public companies in the same industry. For example, if a public company in your industry has a total market valuation (based on its stock price) of 10 times its EBITDA, this multiplier could be the starting point in determining the appropriate multiplier.*

> *This multiplier would then be discounted by the fact that your company was smaller and has less market dominance.*

Many business owners incorrectly assume that the multipliers applicable to larger companies in the industry apply to their smaller company. The multipliers for less dominant companies in an industry are significantly smaller than for dominant companies. [40]

The multiplier used for your company will depend much upon whether you sell during a buyer's or seller's market, as is explained in Chapter Two of this book.

Below is one author's (Rick Rickertsen [41]) view of the different levels of multipliers to be applied to adjusted EBITDA.

EXAMPLE OF EBITDA MULTIPLIERS

Option	Multiple
Strategic Buyer	8-10x
Private Equity (Financial Buyer)	6-8x
Management Buyout (MBO)	5-7x
ESOP	5-6x

This topic should be discussed by the members of The Success Team™ in order to find the estimated multipliers relevant to your business during the exit planning process.

ADJUSTED EBITDA AND THE VALUATION CALCULATION

The following is a fictitious illustration of ABC Example Company, Inc. The Success Team™ has worked together to find the adjustments to EBITDA and the appropriate estimated multiplier. They have already calculated EBITDA and will begin to add or subtract the adjustments. They will then use the agreed-upon estimated multiplier of five times adjusted EBITDA to arrive at the estimated value of the business.

Adjusted EBITDA and the Valuation Calculation

DESCRIPTION	AMOUNT
EBITDA	**$795,000**
Additions:	
Legal, reorganization, audit and appraisal costs to prepare for the sale	165,000
Salaries of family members that will not continue with the buyer	125,000
One-time bonuses paid for a nonrecurring and unusual transaction	75,000
Officer life and disability insurance that will not continue after the sale	25,000
Legal and other costs to buy out a minority owner of the company	80,000
Country club fees and season tickets to the Chicago Cubs	25,000
Vehicles, education and other expenses for three family members	45,000
Deductions:	
Increase in the cost of the person that will replace the owner/manager	(50,000)
Rent paid to the owner below market value for an equivalent building	(45,000)
Below-market salaries paid to key employees to continue with the buyer	(40,000)
Adjusted EBITDA	**$1,200,000**
Multiplier	5x
Estimated value of ABC Example Company, Inc.	**$6,000,000**

Remember, this is a preliminary valuation based upon adjusted EBITDA. There might be many things that can be done to improve upon this amount.

EBITDA VALUATION PERIODS

The Success Team™ will need to discuss the periods of time for the adjusted EBITDA calculations. There are several options:

- The past 36 months
- Trailing 24-month period
- Trailing 12-month period
- Weighted three-year period

It is highly recommended that you begin the process of calculating the current value of your company immediately.

We now want to discuss the ways in the next chapter by which you might increase the value of the company before it is presented to potential buyers.

Chapter 5

Increasing the Value of Your Business

*The number one reason our deals get delayed or don't happen is **declining financial performance**. While due diligence is important, and deals blow up in due diligence, it's not the number one reason for delays or blow ups. In rough percentages, the reasons deals are delayed or don't happen are as follows: (1) Declining financial performance (80%), (2) Unresolved issues that pop up in due diligence (10%) and (3) Owners getting cold feet and backing out (10%).*

Larry Reinharz, Managing Director, Woodbridge International

THE BIG PICTURE

"Brevity is the soul of wit," said Shakespeare in *Hamlet*. His statement rings true with a brief but brilliant statement documented in the previous chapter:

> *For each $1 that you increase your EBITDA during the valuation year, you should arguably receive an additional $4 to $6 in sale price.*
>
> Frederick H. Lipman [42]

The above principle is used in the example below.

Let's use the example in the previous chapter and assume that you and *The Success Team™* of ABC Example Company, Inc. have gone through our process to increase the adjusted EBITDA from $1.2M to $2.2M. Assuming the same multiplier, the before and after values would be as follows:

DESCRIPTION	BEFORE	AFTER
Adjusted EBITDA	$1,200,000	$2,200,000
Multiplier	5x	5x
Estimated value of ABC Example Company, Inc.	$6,000,000	**$11,000,000**

The above example illustrates the purpose of this chapter. We will discuss some of the principles of increasing adjusted EBITDA. This should be one of the highest priorities of *The Success Team™*.

BEING PROACTIVE

The best attitude to take is that you have significant control over the future value of your company.

> *There are measures you can take to increase the value of your business when a sale is imminent – within 18 months or so. There are ways to increase your payday, by millions of dollars in many cases. Just as importantly, there are methods of transforming a marginal business into a saleable one.*
>
> John H. Brown [43]

MINIMIZING DISTRACTIONS

We introduced this topic in an earlier chapter of this book, quoting the successful founder & CEO of *Crate and Barrel*:

> *Getting distracted is the biggest problem entrepreneurs face.*
> *Gordon Segal* [44]

Below is a story about an owner who was excited about getting a check for $40M at the close of the sale. He became distracted during the process. The sale not only fell through but he was left with $750,000 in expenses from the failed transaction, plus some other unexpected and unpleasant problems.

> *Chambers stared into the eyes in the mirror. What the hell had gone wrong? Nine months after signing that lovely agreement, all was dashed. The 40 million bucks. The vacation. The retirement party. The graceful exit into the sunset. Gone.*
>
> *Heaven could wait. He was in hell.*
>
> *Not only was his $40 million deal deader than Napoleon, but there was much worse news. He had taken his eye off the business to work on the deal, and now the company desperately needed his attention. Dealmaking had been **a massive distraction**. Instead of focusing on his customers, he was off meeting in mahogany conference rooms with legal eagles and Turnbull & Associates –clad investment bankers. While Chambers was dealmaking and dreaming about how he would spend his part of the 40 million, sales were falling and profits were down. And, with the worst possible timing, his biggest customer had filed for Chapter 11. He had thought that the new owner could worry about ramping up the business again. **Now he was the new owner.***
>
> *To add insult to injury, like the father of the bride when the groom changed his mind on the way to the altar, Chambers still had to pay the wedding expenses. He was the proud owner of $750,000 in broken deal expenses, $300,000 of which was owed to his law firm.* [45]

Now is the time for you to make a list of the activities and attributes that will help minimize the future distractions. Below is the pyramid of **B2B CFO®** Finders, Minders and Grinders™.[46] It shows a Finder being pulled down to Minding and Grinding activities. The goal during this process is to help you to remove yourself as much as possible from Minding and Grinding activities.

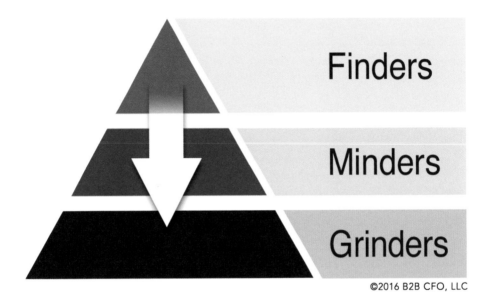

©2016 B2B CFO, LLC

Finders demonstrate some specific attributes that are essential to success. There are numerous terms that can describe the leadership of a Finder:

- *Visionary*
- *Idea generator*
- *Innovator or dreamer*
- *Catalyst for future change*
- *Relationship builder*

You will notice that all of the above attributes or functions require "future" action. Hence, Finders are all about the future. [47]

Below are some ideas to assist in avoiding distractions and to move forward to the future:

- Delegate as much as possible to *The Success Team*™.
- Hold the individual members of *The Success Team*™ accountable.
- Fire and replace unproductive members of *The Success Team*™.
- Work as if the sales transaction will fall through.
- Work up to the day of the close.
- Remain the innovator, the dreamer, the visionary and the idea generator.
- Try to keep your Finding Activities to 70% or more of your time.
- Set realistic goals and start the process to achieve those goals.
- Ask a trusted advisor to immediately tell you if they feel you are getting too distracted.
- Never quit.

Success usually goes to those who never quit.

> *Never give in. Never give in. Never, never, never, never — in nothing, great or small, large or petty — never give in, except to convictions of honor and good sense.*
> *Winston Churchill, October 29, 1941*

> *It is tempting to quit too early. Too often a business owner will travel 90% of the journey and then sell the business. Yet, there is a strong possibility that the value earned during the last 10% of the journey could be worth more than the first 90%.* [48]

The idea is to move most of your time during the exit strategy process from Minding and Grinding into Finding activities, as is illustrated on the next page.

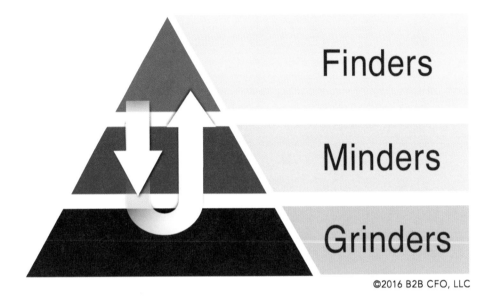

INCREASING SALES AND SALES DIVERSIFICATION

We cannot stress enough how important it is that you continue to operate your company as if no sale were pending. Why? Sales fall through. Given the possibility that you may own your company longer than you anticipated, it makes sense for you to keep it running as profitably as possible.

John H. Brown [49]

The graph on the next page compares periods of time during the exit strategy process. It shows trends of sales and adjusted EBITDA. It compares the **desirable** to the **undesirable** trends.

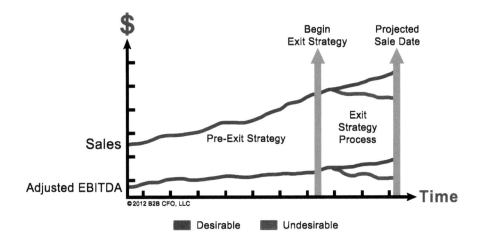

There is a significant difference between being the visionary who causes sales to increase and being involved in the day-to-day sales process. Most buyers view the latter as highly negative.

> *Your job as an entrepreneur is to hire salespeople to sell your products and services so you can spend your time selling your company.*
>
> *An acquirer will want to see that you have a product or service that can be sold by salespeople in general and not just one superstar salesperson.*
>
> *John Warrillow* [50]

Your job as a visionary is to be the catalyst to increase future sales. It is also to see if the company can diversify its sales. This may cause investment of time in software, research and development and in building a more competent sales process.

You want and need your company to do better than whatever your competition is doing. You have the innate God-given talent. Now is the time to see if you have the fire-in-the-belly to be the catalyst for future change.

It is important to remember that **you are the person who will benefit the most** when you cause sales to increase during the exit strategy process.

IMPROVING PROCESSES AND EFFICIENCIES

Increasing and diversifying sales is not the end-all solution to improve the opportunity to sell the company. Efforts must be made to improve certain processes and efficiencies. You and *The Success Team*™ want to focus on the desirable line of the adjusted EBITDA section of the graph below.

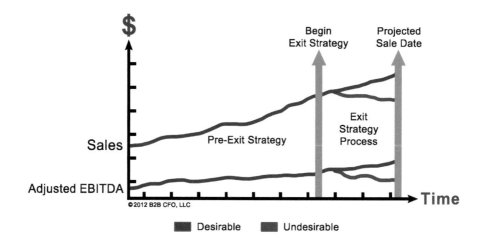

Below is a comparison of how *Business A* was able to keep focused, but simultaneously *Business B* lost focus.

> *Business A and Business B each have $3 million of EBITDA, are located in the same city and are in the same business.*
>
> *Business A has a strong management team motivated by an economic incentive to both improve company performance and remain through any ownership transition. Business A has developed and documented various systems designed to sustain the growth of the business apart from its owner. It has carefully diversified its customer base in the years leading up to the sale process: no customer represents more than 8 percent of its revenue.*
>
> *Business B has a good management team, but they are the same age as the owner and have expressed a desire to leave the business when he does. The company's systems are not*

documented; rather they are "between the ears" of the management team. Business B has six customers.

Which company is worth more*? Which would you pay more for?* [51]

Frederick D. Lipman explained the following factors that influence valuations. Some include the subject of increased revenues and some involve improvements of processes and efficiencies. [52]

Factors Increasing Valuation	Factors Decreasing Valuation
Strong customer relationships on all levels	Weak customer relationships and frequent turnover
Proprietary products or services	Lack of proprietary products or services
No single customer accounts for more than 5% of revenues or profits	A single customer accounts for over 15% of revenues or profits
Strong management team (important to financial buyers)	A weak management team (so-called "one-man-show syndrome")
Excellent employee turnover and relations	Poor employee turnover and relations
Consistent revenue and earnings trends	Inconsistent revenue and earnings trends
Plant and equipment in good repair	Plant or equipment has been neglected and requires significant repairs
Intellectual property assets, which are legally protected	Lack of legally protected intellectual property assets

Some of the improvements in efficiencies and processes might include someone on The Success Team™ overseeing detailed analysis of:

- Sales prices charged to customers
- Discounts given to customers
- Payroll and payroll-related expenses
- Gross profit margin
- Cost of sales
- Fixed expenses
- Variable expenses
- Discounts available from vendors

You want and need to do better than whatever your competition is doing. For example:

> Owners who focus on maximizing their company's gross margins often unlock substantial value. By definition, this means maximizing cost of goods sold. The best investment most owners can make is upgrading the company's purchasing function. Professional materials management pays for itself many times over and helps create market value. Companies can benefit greatly from installing cutting-edge inventory management and other throughput management systems. [53]

AN EXAMPLE

Below is a copy of the table used at the beginning of this chapter.

DESCRIPTION	BEFORE	AFTER
Adjusted EBITDA	$1,200,000	$2,200,000
Multiplier	5x	5x
Estimated value of ABC Example Company, Inc.	$6,000,000	$11,000,000

Let's assume the "after" column increase in adjusted EBITDA is due mostly to your efforts in increasing sales and from creating new sales through diversification. Let's use the amounts in the "After" column and assume some improvements in processes and efficiencies. The table below shows the possible effects of improvements in processes and efficiencies in categories of percentages from 10% to 20%.

DESCRIPTION	10%	15%	20%
Adjusted EBITDA	$2,200,000	$2,200,000	$2,200,000
Increase in adjusted EBITDA due to improvements in processes and efficiencies	10%	15%	20%
Adjusted EBITDA, increased to	$2,420,000	$2,530,000	$2,640,000
Multiplier	5x	5x	5x
Estimated value of ABC Example Company, Inc.	$12,100,00	$12,650,000	$13,200,000

Imagine the value you might be able to add to your company with a combination of increases in sales and improvements in processes and efficiencies!

It is highly recommended that you ask the members of The Success Team™ to give ideas and suggestions to help your company improve its processes and efficiencies. A plan should then be implemented to achieve those ideas.

BRANDING

Branding is complementary to the subject of increasing and diversifying sales. An objective review of your company's brand as it compares to the competition might be a good subject for The Success Team™. You might consider hiring a marketing company that has a good reputation for evaluation and creating brands and branding solutions. As an example, our principle brand, the B2B CFO GamePlan®, is on the next page. It clearly helps separate our company from the competition. Very few words need to be stated when people see our brand. People easily understand what we do and what makes us different from everyone else.

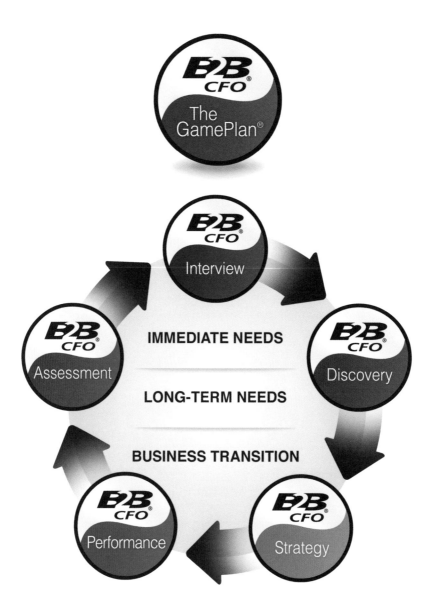

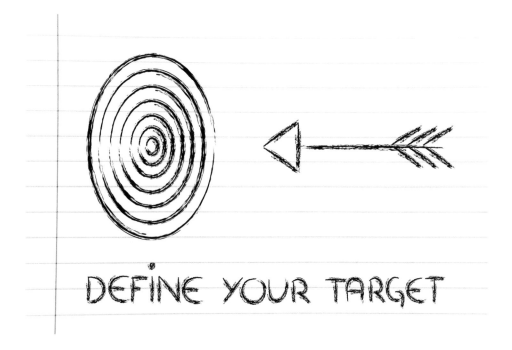

DEFINE YOUR TARGET

Chapter 6

Preparing for Your Last Customer:
The Buyer

A well-prepared business gets more offers, and usually better offers, than does a less-prepared one. A well-prepared business also advances the sale more quickly.

Chances are your business can be improved in ways that enhance a buyer's confidence. The more comfort and trust the buyer has in you and your business, the fewer opportunities a buyer has to question various aspects of the business and negotiate a lower price.

Thomas W. Lyons [54]

You'd never sell your products or services without understanding what your customers want. The same goes for your company: to maximize value, you have to know what they want.

Robert W. Scarlata [55]

THE BIG PICTURE

Your attitude toward the subject in this and the subsequent chapters will make or break your ability to sell your business and to sell it at the value you want.

Depending upon your attitude, this may be the most frustrating or the most interesting process you have gone through so far in your career as an entrepreneur.

The reason for this possible frustration can be summed up in two words: **Due diligence**.

Due diligence will either make or break any future sale of your business. The purpose of this chapter is to help you understand the process so you can move forward to success.

DUE DILIGENCE

Few buyers will purchase a business without conducting an extensive investigation, generally called due diligence. The key to surviving the buyer's due diligence is understanding what areas of your business the buyer is likely to investigate and being prepared for that investigation.

Frederick D. Lipman [56]

The purpose of due diligence on the part of the buyer is to validate the information you've provided to a point where the buyer feels reasonably comfortable and understands the risks involved in the purchase. In virtually every transaction, the buyer's offer is contingent upon the results of the due diligence process.

John F. Dini [57]

The due diligence checklists provided by the buyer can easily have 200-300 individual items to be answered. Below are just 19 of 186 questions asked on an actual due diligence checklist.

		Financial Statements and Overall Financial Review
1		Provide copies of the monthly internal financial reports for the last three years and year-to-date.
	a.	Provide copies of the monthly internal financial reports for the trailing twelve months.
	b.	If any of the internal financial statements provided do not agree to the Audited/Reviewed financial statements, please provide reconciliations for all periods.
2		Copies of Audited/Reviewed financial statements for 2008, 2009, 2010
3		Provide copies of the budgeted financial statements & management projected financial statements for the last three years and the current year. If the budgets were not prepared in the same reporting format as the Company's reviewed or internally prepared financial statements, please provide reconciliations for all years presented. Include detail by customer and by location. Include balance sheet, income statement and cashflow statements
4		Provide written description of budget process
5		Provide Sales ($) and Gross Margin ($ and %) and EBITDA ($ and %) history for 2008, 2009 and 2010
	a.	Location
	b.	Machine
	c.	Service
	d.	Customers
6		Provide copies of the Company's latest business plan/strategic plan, if prepared.
7		Provide Sales $ by calendar month by top 10 customers, location and service categories for 2008, 2009 and 2010
8		Gross margin analysis (components of COGS) for 2008-2010 by month
9		Components of employee costs by function and type (salary, bonus, benefits, etc) for 2008-2010 by month
10		Provide monthly letters of credit outstanding 2008-2010
11		Provide copies of the Company's detailed trial balance as of the years ended 2008, 2009, and 2010.
12		Capital expenditure breakdown/requirements 2008-2010 and projections for 2011 (including maintenance vs. growth expenditures).
13		Provide interim financials
	a.	Detail and summary trial balances
	b.	Detail report of all accrued expenses and other liabilities
	c.	Roll-forward of bad debt calculation
14		Provide examples/copies of any reports management reviews on a daily, weekly, monthly or annual basis to understand the business.
15		Provide detailed listing of company owned stock or other investments
16		Provide a description of any other assets or notes receivable on the balance sheet.
17		Provide a copy of bank reconciliations for most recent month
18		Provide a list of all outstanding bonds
19		Discuss profitability as it relates to fuel prices

Owners are usually not prepared for the wide-ranging and numerous questions to be answered during this process, which may become difficult for some owners, such as the following story.

DUE DILIGENCE GONE BAD

The example below is not unusual and can be used as a learning curve that should be avoided during this process.

"The stream turns into a torrent."

A successful exit is seldom spontaneous, but the result of a carefully prepared process.

The following scene has been played out countless times: an investor approaches the business owner with an offer that seems attractive. They go out for a wonderful lunch or dinner – the great seduction scene. The personal chemistry is excellent, consensus emerges quickly, and the parties map out a deal on the back of a napkin. They shake hands on the general framework of a deal, perhaps even agree on the value of the business, and depart thinking that the deal is done, subject only to some minor details.

Then the investor starts with his or her Due Diligence. A trickle of questions turns into an endless stream. One set of answers leads to another set of questions. The stream turns into a torrent. The barrage of questions puts serious pressure on company management. The investor becomes frustrated with the slow pace at which the incomplete information is provided, and with the ambiguity or inaccuracy, or perhaps even contradictory nature, of the information received. The owner becomes frustrated with the resources consumed, and often misconstrues the questions as a lack of trust or failing commitment on the part of the investor. If the initial waves of questions are answered satisfactorily, the investor goes on to appoint legal advisors and auditors, who then unleash further extensive waves of newer and even more complicated and more detailed questions. Whole teams of advisors descend upon the company, taking information demands to new heights. Company management is under huge stress – after all, managers have a business to run, yet satisfying the investor turns into more than a full-time job. Tensions mount. More often than not, negotiations break off – sometimes in an emotional or dramatic showdown – or the parties may just give up from exhaustion or frustration. [58]

THE ADVANCED DUE DILIGENCE PROCESS™

The B2B CFO® process advances due diligence.

Most due diligence is done after a potential buyer has made a preliminary offer. The due diligence process then begins, usually with **a very short time frame allowed to the seller**. The seller then needs to quickly provide either thousands or tens of thousands of documents under much duress. The seller is also required to invest thousands of man-hours by the owner, management, employees, attorneys and other professionals. The cost of the due diligence to the seller can easily run into six figures. This six-figure amount is usually unbudgeted and can put a significant financial strain on the company's operational cash.

> *Most owners are shocked by the depth and breadth of the due diligence process. This process of "full and fair" disclosure enables a buyer to verify all provided data and reviews all information about the company. "All" includes anything that would interest the buyer at any level.*
>
> *Most business owners are highly independent people who find this disclosure process extremely uncomfortable.* [59]

As a result of constant distractions and time requirements, more often than not, sales and adjusted EBITDA start going down, as illustrated in the graph.

The distractions in "the stream turns into a torrent" story above are usually the reasons for the "undesirable" results illustrated in the above graph.

73

The Advanced Due Diligence Process™ has been created to help you with the preparation process before the buyer is approached. Assuming a future buyer's market, you want your company to be better prepared than any other company the buyer might be looking to purchase.

A BUYER'S MARKET

While no guarantees can be made that the buyer will be interested in your business, the principles discussed so far in this chapter indicate that a well-prepared business often has a better chance with a buyer than an unprepared business.

80% to 85% PREPARATION

The goal of the subsequent chapters and *The Advanced Due Diligence Process*™ is not to prepare your company 100% for the due diligence questions to be asked by a potential buyer. That goal is impossible to achieve. All buyers will have their own unique questions, some of which might be specific to an industry.

The goal of *The Advanced Due Diligence Process* ™ is to have your company prepared 80% to 85% for the prospective buyer. This goal will make the process much easier for both you and the buyer. This goal will also separate your company from the competition to the prospective buyer.

For example, assume the buyer is seriously looking at your company and another that the buyer views as "very similar." Let's also assume your company is 85% ready for the buyer and the competing company is only 5% ready. Which company, in this scenario, has the competitive advantage with the buyer?

THE ADVANCED DUE DILIGENCE PROCESS™ IS UNIQUE

There are several factors that make *The Advanced Due Diligence Process™* unique, all of which should work to your advantage:

- The business owner is in control of the entire process at all times.
- Members of *The Success Team™* should work together for the owner's best interest.
- *The Success Team™* allows business owners to delegate specific tasks.
- Our dashboard software allows owners to easily track delegated tasks.
- Company value can be easily updated using our dashboard software.
- The topics of due diligence are categorized into easy-to-use chapters.
- The due diligence items are assigned to specific people with completion dates.
- Each item completed is stored in a Data Room, ready for review by a buyer.
- The due diligence process is completed before approaching a buyer.
- The process can be performed over a reasonable period of time that should not put stress on the owner, the management or the employees of the company.

We can't emphasize enough the importance of using our dashboard software to manage this process. This software is unique and can be a very valuable tool to help achieve your goals.

UNDERSTANDING THE CUSTOMER'S NEEDS

The future buyer of your business should be viewed as a customer.

Successful entrepreneurs are experts at finding the needs of their customers. They will spend significant resources to find the customer's needs in order to fulfill them. These business owners have significant competitive drive to be the first or the best at meeting the customer's needs, partly in order to receive a financial reward but also to be better than the competition.

And so it is with the future potential buyers of your company. One of them will become the future customer. The goal is not only to sell the company but to sell it at the highest possible price. This means there must be a concentrated effort to find the needs of these future customers who might someday bid for the privilege of buying your business.

You want something from your customer, the future buyer: **_A very large check_**.

Your future customer, the buyer, wants something from you: **_Information_**.

The balance of this book is to help you prepare the information the future buyer wants in order to help you get what you want. The following chapters are organized as follows in order to help you give the buyer what they need:

- The Data Room Checklist
- General Information Checklist
- Management and Employees Checklist
- Product or Service Lines Checklist
- Competition Checklist
- Customer Information Checklist
- Key Vendors and Service Providers Checklist
- Intellectual Property and Intangible Assets Checklist
- Technology, Software and Hardware Checklist
- Branding, Marketing and Public Relations Checklist

- Related Parties and Minority Owners Checklist
- Insurance Checklist
- Internal Financial Statements Checklist
- Inventory Checklist
- External Financial Statements Checklist
- Contracts and Leases Checklist
- Litigation and Claims Checklist
- Taxes Checklist
- Environmental Checklist

A SUGGESTED APPROACH

The beginning of this process may seem overwhelming. After all, you still have a business to run, customers to satisfy, payroll to meet, and a myriad of other short-term and long-term tasks.

Remembering an adage might be appropriate as you gaze into the future on this new venture:

"When eating an elephant take one bite at a time."
Creighton Williams Abrams Jr.

The Advanced Due Diligence Process™ documented in the remaining chapters of this book contains 200-plus individual tasks. You might consider the following approach after assembling the members of *The Success Team*™:

- Meet with the *Team Manager* to determine which topics should be assigned to others.
- The *Team Manager* should work with those assigned to determine which items are "not applicable" to your company. For example, your company may or may not have to do any or all of the nine tasks on the *Environmental* checklist.
- Have the *Team Manager* go into our dashboard software to mark the "not applicable" items. Our dashboard database will then calculate the number of items that are possibly open for your company. This will give you and *The Success Team*™ a better idea of the scope and the number of tasks that need to be completed during this process.
- The *Team Manager* should prioritize those tasks that are long term and short term.

- Specific tasks should be assigned by the owner and *Team Manager* with specific due dates.
- Those assigned specific due dates should be held accountable for completion.
- Have the *Team Manager* report to you regularly.
- Meet regularly with *The Success Team*™.
- Use our dashboard software to regularly check the progress of the tasks.

Now, onto the next chapter, which is about the importance of the Data Room.

Chapter 7

The Data Room

One of the most important steps of *The Advanced Due Diligence Process*™ is the location of the documents that will be created or prepared for the future buyer to view. This chapter will discuss some of the options available as well as some of the serious concerns about this process.

The location of the due diligence documents is commonly known as the Data Room.

Control over the disclosure of this information is critical. This is, after all, your information and nobody has a right to see it until you give the approval. The Data Room will contain many of your company's most important documents. It may contain trade secrets and other information that makes your company unique. Formality is important in this step and working with the attorney and other members of *The Success Team*™ is paramount.

> *Your transaction attorney should control disclosure of documents and information.*
>
> *John H. Brown* [60]

OVERVIEW

Let's assume the role is reversed and you are going to purchase a company. Both you and the seller would sign the appropriate nondisclosure and other legally-binding documents provided by the attorneys. You would then have the expectation that you and your team (anyone you wish) would have access to the seller's documents. You would assume that the location should be easily accessible. You should also have privacy when you and your team discuss the documents provided.

Your prospective buyers will have the same expectations from you during this process.

> *It is customary to maintain a data room in which all relevant documentation about the seller can be inspected by the potential buyer or buyers who are performing due diligence.*
> *Frederick D. Lipman* [61]

The volume of the documents that will be stored in your Data Room may surprise you. Careful thought will need to be given about the location of these documents.

> *Depending upon the size and complexity of the company being sold, the Data Room may contain thousands or even hundreds of thousands of documents, including all relevant client, supplier, employee, financing, and other contracts, as well as title documents, board minutes and so on. Indeed, any document that could have an impact on the value of the company should be in the Data Room.*
> *Les Nemethy* [62]

> *Into this room go copies of every relevant document needed to review the deal. More documents are pulled in by the barrelful during the process. These include primary customer contracts, primary supply contracts, leases, lawsuits, articles of incorporation, insurance documents, 401K plans, all audits for the past four years, primary management reports, employment contracts, and recent industry analyses. This room becomes the center of the deal, with auditors, lawyers, investment partners, and others buzzing like bees around a hive.*
> *Rick Rickertsen* [63]

SECURITY AND SETTING THE RULES

Security of these documents should be one of the first topics discussed by *The Success Team*™. The topic of security does not always extend solely to the prospective buyer. There are sometimes serious issues related to exposing certain documents to:

- Employees
- Certain members of management
- Some family members
- Hostile minority owners
- Etc.

It is important to remember that most deals fall through. *The Success Team*™ wants to keep this perspective and a thorough discussion of any individuals that should be limited to certain documents needs to be explored. You should share your concerns with *The Success Team*™ and they should do likewise with you.

> *In a physical Data Room, the seller's representative is usually present at all times to ensure that only authorized personnel from the investors are in attendance, that no one is making unauthorized copies or scans of information, and that legitimate information requests are coordinated.* **A Data Room is often governed by rules set by the seller**, *which the investors must sign or acknowledge in order to gain access.* [64]

DATA ROOM OPTIONS

Your company has options for the physical location of the Data Room. Some of those options might include the following, all of which have positives and negatives to be discussed by *The Success Team*™:

- Your company's location
- The offices of an attorney
- A Virtual Data Room

YOUR COMPANY'S LOCATION

The quality of a Data Room, and how the process is managed, can make or break a sale process. It can also dramatically affect valuation, as investors often use shortcomings in the Data Room to drive down prices. [65]

It may seem like a simple decision to keep the documents for the Data Room at your company's location. That may be in your best interest. Below are some issues that you and *The Success Team*™ should consider regarding this matter:

- Can the Data Room be secured at all times, 24/7/365, and in such a way that nobody can enter the room, other than those you specifically want?
- Is the room large enough to have many secured file cabinets to contain the information? (Remember, the file cabinets may need to contain thousands of documents).
- Is there enough space for many people to work simultaneously in the room for many days? The room may need to contain a large conference table and adequate space for up to a dozen or more people working at any one given time.
- Is the room large enough to have a photocopier, scanner and computer equipment?
- Does the room have capacity for people to access the Internet?
- Is there someone in your company that you can trust to secure the safety of the documents? If not, are you willing to hire such a person?
- Do you have a competent employee who is organized enough to know where documents have been filed, how to immediately retrieve the documents, and how to properly store them after retrieval?
- Does your company employ a person bold enough to not let investors and others make unauthorized copies or scans of certain documents?
- What will it cost to insure the documents?
- What is the backup plan in the case of a fire or theft?
- What is the total estimated cost of having an on-site Data Room?

One of the most important issues to consider with an on-site Data Room is the impression it will make upon current and future employees. They will see a dozen or more "three-piece-suits" coming and going into the

Data Room. That sight will leave a certain impression upon employees. They are, after all, very concerned about their jobs and will wonder if something is wrong with the company. Some will be smart or experienced enough to figure out what is going on — you are about to sell the company. This may cause problems that you had not anticipated, such as certain employees unexpectedly exiting the company before the transaction closes. These may be some of the employees that you told the potential buyer are important for the future success of the company. There is another very important issue related to those three-piece-suits. One would expect that they would always be professional and always stay within the boundaries agreed upon prior to beginning the due diligence process in the Data Room. Naturally, the three-piece-suits are human beings and are often curious about things outside of the Data Room. They may wander around the factory, plant or offices in an unannounced and unauthorized manner. You can always call your attorney and try to keep the "suits" in line, but they may have already caused problems you are not even aware of at the time.

THE OFFICES OF AN ATTORNEY

You may wish to keep the Data Room at an attorney's office. The key factors are:

- Location
- Cost

The location must be close enough for you, the management team, key employees and others to quickly go to the Data Room to answer questions and to make explanations from the buyer's representatives. Time will be of the essence during this process. Many unplanned trips to the Data Room may be required to work with the buyer's representatives and a good location will be important to you and your team.

> *During the Data Room process, you and your advisors must be prepared to answer questions and provide supplementary information to investors. Answers are mostly expected within one or two days, failing which investors may ask for an extension of the period during which the Data Room is open. It may be necessary to disclose additional documents beyond what was originally contained in the Data Room.* [66]

You should receive a written estimate of the cost of keeping the Data Room at an attorney's office. The cost may be significant. It might include:

- Space
- Filing of the documents
- An attorney or paralegal present during the times the buyer's representatives are in the room
- Copies or scans for the buyer
- Etc.

VIRTUAL DATA ROOM

The Success Team™ may want to consider using a Virtual Data Room (VDR) instead of a typical physical location. Some of the key issues for *The Success Team*™ related to a discussion and research of the viability of a VDR are:

- Security
- VDR to be cloud-based or hosted on a local server
- Scanning documents into the VDR
- Validating that each scanned document is properly stored on the VDR
- The process of allowing the buyer access to the data
- Backup redundancy for all documents
- The cost

Below is a description of the VDR and some possible benefits, assuming certain legal and security measures are in place and enforceable.

> *A virtual data room (sometimes called a VDR) is an online repository of information that is used for the storing and distribution of documents. In many cases, a virtual data room is used to facilitate the due diligence process. This due diligence process has traditionally used a physical data room to accomplish the disclosure of documents. For reasons of cost, efficiency and security, virtual data rooms have widely replaced the more traditional physical data room.*

> *An alternative to the physical data room involves the setting up of a virtual data room in the form of an extranet to which the bidders and their advisers are given access via the Internet. An extranet*

is essentially an Internet site with limited controlled access, using a secure log-on supplied by the vendor, which can be disabled at any time, by the vendor if a bidder withdraws. Much of the information released is confidential and restrictions are applied to the viewer's ability to release this to third parties (by means of forwarding, copying or printing). This can be effectively applied to protect the data using Digital Rights Management.

In the process of Mergers & Acquisitions, the data room is set up as part of the central repository of data relating to companies or divisions being acquired or sold. The data room enables the interested parties to view information relating to the business in a controlled environment. Confidentiality is paramount and strict controls for viewing, copying and printing are imposed. Conventionally this is achieved by establishing a supervised, physical data room in secure premises with controlled access. In most cases, with a physical data room, only one bidder team can access the room at a time. This becomes time consuming.

A virtual data room has exactly the same strengths as a conventional data room — controlling access, viewing, copying and printing as well as setting time limits on viewing and logging. It has none of the disadvantages of being in a standard location, needing couriers to move documents or transporting of key staff and personnel back and forth. It is also accessible 24/7 over the allowed period. With a virtual data room, documents reach the regulators and investors in a more efficient and timely manner.

A virtual data room is quick to set up. Scanned data and existing electronic files can be mixed, information can be added or eliminated at any time (the changes could be logged if required) and any or all information can be restricted to any or all registered viewers at any time. [67]

This book does not totally agree with all of the advantages listed above. Some of these ideas are subject to analysis because each company that sells is unique. The above information is shared to help *The Success Team*™ in gaining knowledge about VDRs. There may be significant risks involved with a VDR and caution is warranted with this decision.

A PHYSICAL AND A VIRTUAL DATA ROOM

It may be to your advantage to consider using a combination of both a physical and a VDR.

> *Sometimes the parties opt for a combination of virtual and physical Data Rooms, with the most confidential documents appearing only in the physical Data Room. One advantage of many virtual Data Rooms is that it is possible to monitor who was accessing what documents at what time (e.g., to what degree each investor is taking seriously the Due Diligence process).* [68]

This is an important decision, but you have adequate time to think this over and to make plans.

It is now time to begin *The Advanced Due Diligence Process*™.

"*The Exit Strategy Handbook* closes the mental gap between the business owner and the Investment Banking community."

Henry Dubroff, Founder and Editor, Pacific Coast Business Times

The Advanced Due Diligence Process™

The next 18 chapters explain our process. The information in the checklists in these chapters is also in our dashboard software.

Chapter 8
General Information Checklist

The prospective buyer wants to learn some very general information about your company in order to begin their due diligence process.

Legal Structure – Document the company's organization chart, including any wholly-owned or partially-owned subsidiaries. These subsidiaries may be owned by you or by the company or by other owners in the company. They will want complete information about these subsidiaries. It will be important to let them know if any of these subsidiaries will not be a part of the sales transaction. This information should include articles of incorporation, bylaws and complete operating agreements. Your company should disclose any DBA (doing business as), AKA (also known as) or any other fictitious name filings. This information should include any name changes of the company during any of the past 10 years.

Minutes – Some closely-held companies are not detailed about keeping minutes or corporate resolutions, even if the state statutes require the maintenance of the minutes. You may want to go over the minutes with your attorney if there is anything sensitive that is in the minutes and/or needs more explanation. The buyer is looking at the minutes and corporate resolutions in an attempt to discover certain past transactions, such as the purchase of a subsidiary, issuance of stock or ownership, lawsuits, claims, employee dispute matters, purchases of equipment, related party transactions, etc. Consider asking your attorney to write a memorandum to be placed in the minute book in the event the company does not have adequate minutes or resolutions as required by any state statutory or regulatory authority. The buyer will want to see documents for the past five years.

Stock Certificates – The buyer will want to see a lot of documentation if your company is a corporation regardless of whether it files income taxes on a C-corporation or S-corporation basis. They are keenly interested to see who might have any ownership or ownership rights in the stock of the company. This list would include current stock owners, prior stock owners, stock transfer certificates, stock options, stock rights, etc. They will also want to see any agreement relating to voting rights, registration rights, preemptive rights, rights of first refusal or option rights.

Membership Interests – Some closely-held companies operate as limited liability companies and/or partnerships. The buyer will want to see a list of the members or partners of the company including any and all rights of the members or partners, especially as it relates to transfer of interest rights.

Foreign Countries – It is common today for closely-held companies to have ownership interests and/or registrations and licenses to do business in foreign countries. It is important to document and disclose agreements with foreign countries, investors, vendors, manufacturers, etc. This would include any agreements that are in progress and not yet completed.

Buy-Sell Agreements – Many closely-held companies have buy-sell agreements with co-owners or with subsidiaries owned by the company. It is important to disclose all buy-sell agreements, even those with owners who are no longer employees of the company.

General Information
Checklist

#	Subject	Description	n/a	Assigned To	Expected Completion Date	Completed & in the Data Room
1	Structure	A diagram of the organizational structure of the company and any subsidiaries or affiliates, including percentage ownership of voting securities of any subsidiaries				
2	Articles, Bylaws	Articles or certificates of incorporation or organization including bylaws and operating agreements of the company and any subsidiary as originally filed				
3	Name Changes	List the original name of the company and any name changes during the past 10 years				
4	Names	A schedule of the names and resumes of the current officers, directors and other key employees of the company				
5	Minutes	Minutes, resolutions and written consents of shareholders, directors and officers for the past five years				
6	Stock, Owners	Copy of the stock ledger and stock transfer certificates. List of all owners of the company				

General Information
Checklist
(continued)

#	Subject	Description	n/a	Assigned To	Expected Completion Date	Completed & in the Data Room
7	Foreign	List of foreign countries in which the company and its subsidiaries are authorized or registered to do business				
8	Agree-ment	Any agreement related to voting, issuance of equity, registration rights, preemptive rights, rights of first refusal, or option rights of the company and its subsidiaries				
9	Buy-Sell	Copy of all buy-sell agreements and any owner agreements				
10	Options	A schedule of all options, warrants, rights, and any other potentially dilutive securities with exercise prices and vesting options				
11	DBA & AKA	List any DBA (doing business as), AKA (also known as) and any fictitious name filings for the past 10 years				
12	Locations	List all locations the company has operated in during the past 10 years				

General Information
Checklist
(continued)

#	Subject	Description	n/a	Assigned To	Expected Completion Date	Completed & in the Data Room
13	Rights	List the rights of each class of stock or owner's interests				
14	Number	List the number of authorized and issued stock or owner's interests				

Chapter 9

Management and Employees Checklist

Key People – Key personnel and management are often one of the most important assets of the company. The buyer will want to see detailed and current resumes on these people in order to assess which, if any, of these employees will be given an offer to continue with the buyer after the close of the transaction. In addition to current resumes, it is important to provide current compensation, bonus packages, employment contracts, buy-sell agreements, documentation of any oral promises or contracts, and any equity compensation packages. Employees who have been with the company for a long time often need to update their resumes to show the history and responsibilities they have had since being employed with your company. All of the above would be applicable to any key personnel or management of any subsidiaries that will become a part of the sales transaction.

Directors – Document the names of any members of a Board of Directors or an Executive Committee, including any form of compensation including stock options, equity options, trade outs, or any types of promised compensation. These people are sometimes given other perks or benefits that need to be documented, such as health insurance, automobiles, discounts on the purchase of the company's products or services, etc. Provide their resumes or URL links to bios.

Employee Manual – Provide a copy of the company's latest employee manual, including any important policies and procedures that are not included in the manual. This documentation should give the prospective buyer information on all benefits of the company, such as vacation and sick leave, Family and Medical Leave Act benefits, jury duty, military leave, leave of absence, health insurance, retirement plan benefits, workers' compensation, disability or life insurance benefits, etc. This information should also include important policies and procedures on sexual harassment, termination of employees, COBRA, etc. You might consider discussing this topic with your attorney if some of the items above are not documented.

Contracts – Many closely-held companies have written or oral contracts with employees. You might want to discuss this topic with your attorney if any important oral contracts are in place at the time of this due diligence process. Contracts with employees might include commission plans, consulting agreements, confidentiality and nondisclosure agreements, compensation agreements, etc.

Benefit Plans – All buyers will want to see the details about any and all benefit plans the company has for its employees. The business reason for this information is to allow the buyers to see if their current benefit plans meet or exceed the plans of your company in the event they want some of the employees to continue with them after the close of the transaction. They will want to see the details behind any Defined Contribution Plans (e.g., 401K, profit sharing, cafeteria plans), Defined Benefit Plans or any other types of plans. They will also want to see any proposed changes to the plans that have been communicated to the employees but are not yet effective.

Management and Employees
Checklist

#	Subject	Description	n/a	Assigned To	Expected Completion Date	Completed & in the Data Room
1	Organization	Management organization chart				
2	Directors	A list of the Board of Directors or Executive Committee. Describe any compensation, stock options, equity or future promised compensation of any kind				
3	Resumes	Current resumes of key management				
4	Key People	Management compensation, bonuses, contracts, compensation equity or future promised compensation				
5	Employee Manual	A copy of the latest employee manual and personnel policy memos not contained in the manual				
6	Leave Policies	Detail any leave policies not in the employee manual (e.g., vacation, sick leave, Family & Medical Leave Act, holidays, jury, military leave, leave of absence)				
7	Benefits & Policies	Describe any benefits (e.g., health insurance, retirement plans, workers compensation, disability) and any policies (e.g., sexual harassment , termination, COBRA) not listed in the employee manual				
8	Register	The latest payroll register for all employees				
9	Hiring, Training	A copy of the hiring and training processes for all employees, including part-time employees				

Management and Employees
Checklist
(continued)

#	Subject	Description	n/a	Assigned To	Expected Completion Date	Completed & in the Data Room
10	Accruals	Detail of all accrued liabilities related to employees (e.g., vacation, sick leave)				
11	Benefit Plans	Summary and copies of benefit plans (e.g., profit sharing, 401(k), cafeteria, Defined Benefit) and details on any potential changes to be made in the future				
12	Contracts	All employee contracts, commission plans, consulting agreements, confidentiality agreements and noncompetition agreements, including a written description of oral contracts or agreements (including part-time employees and consultants)				
13	Compliance	A schedule indicating satisfaction of citizenship requirements, workers compensation claims for the past two years				

Chapter 10

Product and Service Lines Checklist

Comment – The company's product or service lines are usually the most important asset of the company and the key reason the buyer is interested in the possible purchase. It is very important to give a lot of attention to the documentation provided on this checklist to help the buyer understand whether your company stands out from the competition and is a serious contender for the possible sales transaction.

Technology - Divulging trade secrets is a complicated process and discussions should be had with an attorney and *The Success Team*™ before communicating trade secrets about sales and cost of sales to the prospective buyer. That being said, these trade secrets may become one of the company's most important assets and one of the key reasons the prospective buyer might purchase your company instead of one of your competitor's companies. Caution is advised before giving the prospective buyer these trade secrets. A good intellectual property attorney will know how to possibly protect your company with this subject.

Sales – Historical and projected sales of key product or service lines are important. The buyer needs to understand the history behind the sales line items in order to determine if the future projections are realistic.

Much time needs to be given to a written history of the sales and key assumptions for future sales. It is not realistic to assume the buyers know the business as well as you. They need assistance in understanding the sales history and the reasons you feel future sales will be met. Time spent on documentation of these issues is paramount, including any unusual increases or decreases in sales, both historically and in the projections.

Cost of Sales – This is an area in which the prospective buyer is most vulnerable in terms of risk, unless the buyer is an industry expert. The buyer will automatically assume worst-case scenarios unless your company takes adequate time to document certain information, such as the reasons the company's cost of sales might be lower than industry, special discount arrangements with vendors, certain efficiencies due to machinery and equipment, efficiencies with personnel, efficiencies in your company's unique processes, etc. It is equally important to give very detailed written explanations if there have been periods of time that the company experienced higher-than-normal cost of sales, such as in the following example given in a previous chapter in this book.

> *My company negotiated the sale of a business that was operating a large fleet of trucks. Suddenly, fuel prices shot up to unprecedented levels. We assessed the situation and found reason to believe that fuel prices would be more stable in the future. In preparing the profit and loss statement for EBITDA purposes, we recast the most recent fuel costs to more reasonable levels.* [69]

Diversification – The prospective buyer will not only be interested in the most profitable historical sales but will be keenly interested if there are steps in place to diversify revenue streams. Time should be taken to document future possible plans to diversify revenue, which might include items that are in research and development and other steps the company has taken to diversify future sales. Care should be given and discussions with attorneys should be had if any of this information might be considered a trade secret.

Product and Service Lines
Checklist

#	Subject	Description	n/a	Assigned To	Expected Completion Date	Completed & in the Data Room
1	Sales, Cost & Gross Profit	Detail the sales, cost of sales, gross profit and gross profit margin for each material individual product or service type for the past three years				
2	Future	Detail the sales, cost of sales, gross profit and gross profit margin for each material individual product or service type for the next three years				
3	Variances	Explain any key variance in sales, cost of sales, gross profit and gross profit margin for the past three years				
4	Future Variances	Explain any key variance in sales, cost of sales, gross profit and gross profit margin for the next three years				
5	Most Profitable	Identify the sales for product or services that are the most profitable for the company (i.e., gross profit or gross profit margin)				
6	Barriers	Document the key barriers that are stopping the company from increasing sales (or gross profit) on its most profitable product or service lines				
7	Resources	Document current and future resources the company needs to increase sales (or gross profit) on its most profitable product or service lines				

Product and Service Lines
Checklist
(continued)

#	Subject	Description	n/a	Assigned To	Expected Completion Date	Completed & in the Data Room
8	Technology	Identify any technology, patents, copyrights, trademarks, software or any other technology needed to increase sales (or gross profit) on the company's most profitable product or service lines				
9	Diversify	Document new product or service lines that might be more profitable than the company's current most profitable product or service lines, including resources needed for the new product or service lines				
10	Bids	Document the company's current bid or RFP process for all material product or service lines				

Chapter 11

Competition Checklist

Market Share – Document the share of the market owned by your company plus any plans to increase the market share in the near future. Explain the market share owned by your key competition, by name, with the goal of identifying those key competitors that make up a majority of your market. Explain future key competitors that you feel might enter the market and the amount of the market share you feel these key competitors will take away from your company, if any.

Your Advantages – This is an opportunity to explain the advantages your company has in the market. The focal point of this checklist is to document any and all advantages your company has over the competition. It will be a detriment to your company's exit strategy if one of the key advantages is you as the owner. The buyer is interested in running the company in the future without you, so it will be to your advantage to explain how the company might operate without you and why you perceive this as a benefit to the buyer. Advantages might include a combination of things, such as specialized software, technology owned, key people, patents, trademarks, trade secrets, location advantages, brand name recognition, sale price advantages, reasons for any customer loyalty, royalty agreements, franchise agreements, significant contracts or purchase orders with customers or vendors, association with foreign companies, financial resources your company has over the competition, joint venture agreements, covenants not to compete, labor agreements, specialty licenses, etc.

Their Advantages – You and your management team already know the advantages the competition has over your company. This is an opportunity to identify those advantages as well as the resources needed to turn their advantages into your advantages. Some of these opportunities might relate to an investment of money, such as the purchase of certain equipment; the hiring of key people; the purchase or lease of specialized software or hardware; increases in marketing and advertising; hiring a public relations firm; increased exposure on Google and other search engines; inbound marketing campaigns on Facebook, Twitter and other social media; money to complete research; and development that is in process or that should be in process, etc.

Trends – Industries rarely remain static, especially in a global economy. Identify future trends for your industry and how those trends might become an advantage or disadvantage to your company. Document the ways you and your management team have identified important trends in order to overcome or take advantage of these market trends.

Competition
Checklist

#	Subject	Description	n/a	Assigned - To	Expected Completion Date	Completed & in the Data Room
1	Current Competitors	List the top competitors to the company and the approximate percentage of the market owned by them and the company				
2	Future Competitors	List new or future competitors of the company and a projection of the sales that competition might take from the company				
3	Key Basis	Explain the key basis of the competition (e.g., price, service, technology, quality, distribution, location)				
4	Your Advantage	Describe any advantages the company has over the competition (e.g., software, technology, people, patents, trademarks, location, brand name, price advantages, customer loyalty, royalty agreements, significant contracts, foreign associations, financial resources, joint venture or partnership, covenants not to compete, labor agreements, licenses)				
5	Their Advantage	Describe any advantages the competition has over the company (e.g., software, technology, people, patents, trademarks, location, brand name, price advantages, royalty agreements, significant contracts, foreign associations, financial resources, joint venture or partnership, covenants not to compete, labor agreements, licenses)				

Competition
Checklist
(continued)

#	Subject	Description	n/a	Assigned To	Expected Completion Date	Completed & in the Data Room
6	R&D	Describe any research and development (R&D) the company has spent on new product lines or services				
7	Resources	Explain the resources the company needs to gain additional market share from the competition. Explain in detail how the company would take market share away from the competition				
8	Trends	Explain the current and projected market trends of your company's industry				

Chapter 12

Customer Information Checklist

Customer Information – Revealing detailed information about customers is usually a very sensitive issue with business owners. This is natural and you should discuss any concerns with *The Success Team*™. The members of the team might have suggestions to help you before you begin this disclosure process. The buyer wants to gather enough information to determine if the customers will continue to buy from them after the sales transaction. Hence, they will ask for a significant amount of information from your company about the customers.

Sales – Disclose the sales by customer for the past three years. The potential buyer is looking for certain customer trends, especially if those trends would cause saturation by one or more customers. The buyer would like to see that no single customer makes up 5% or more of the sales. The business reason for this criterion is related to risk. The more your company relies on a customer who makes up 5% or more of sales, the more the buyer views that customer as a business risk. The buyer will want to see the top 10 customers who have purchased from you during the past three years. Again, this analysis is related to risk. The buyer wants to see diversification in the customer list. Your company might consider writing an explanation of unusually high sales volume by a single customer or a group of customers and if you feel that trend might reverse itself in the future.

Contracts – Disclose all material (significant) contracts or purchase orders with customers, both current and pending. The buyer will want to see if the customer can continue with them if the sale closes. They will also want to see the specific obligations and commitments that have been made to the customer.

Advertising – Your company's method of advertising to attract customers may be a trade secret, especially if your company is using search engine optimization (SEO) or search engine marketing (SEM) advertising campaigns on search engines. Care should be given to discuss such matters with an intellectual property attorney and *The Success Team*™ before divulging these sales techniques. The buyers will want to learn the details of the advertising techniques and expenditures for the past three years. They will also want to know if your company is in the process of developing new advertising campaigns for the near future.

Credit – Most companies sell on accounts receivable to customers. The buyer will want to know the terms of these sales. The buyer will also want to know the credit approval process for your customers. Provide a copy of the policies and procedures related to extending credit to customers. Explain the policies and procedures related to a customer becoming past due on the amount owed to your company. The buyer will spend a lot of time looking at the accounts receivable aging in order to determine if certain customers are too risky to buy from you.

Customer Information
Checklist

#	Subject	Description	n/a	Assigned To	Expected Completion Date	Completed & in the Data Room
1	Sales	Sales by customer for the past three years				
2	Saturation	List all customers that make up 5% or more of annual sales for the past three years				
3	Top 10	List the top 10 customers during the past three years				
4	Foreign	List all customers that are foreign companies. Include any past foreign currency transaction losses or gains				
5	Contracts	Copies of material contracts or purchaser orders with customers, including any joint venture agreements with current or pending customers				
6	Discounts, Pricing	List material discounts, markdowns or pricing special arrangements with key customers				
7	Warranties	List all product warranties and guarantees made to customers, including warranty costs for the past three years				
8	Selection	Describe the company's selection and targeting process for customers				
9	Advertising	Break down the advertising expenditures for the past three years (e.g., television, radio, yellow pages, Search Engine Optimization, Search Engine Marketing)				
10	New Sales	Describe any new sales initiatives or programs that are under consideration				
11	Financing	Describe and list any customer financing and customer buyback obligations				

Customer Information
Checklist
(continued)

#	Subject	Description	n/a	Assigned To	Expected Completion Date	Completed & in the Data Room
12	Credit	Customer credit policies and the procedures for approving and granting credit to new customers				
13	Backlog	A detail of open sales order backlogs				
14	Terminated	For the past two years, list all customers who constitute 5% or more of sales who have left the company (voluntarily or involuntarily)				
15	Gross Profit	For customers material to total sales, list any material variances of gross profit from the average gross profit of the company				
16	Financial Trouble	Detail any customer who the company feels or knows is in financial trouble				

Chapter 13

Key Vendors and Service Providers Checklist

Key Vendors – The potential buyer may or may not be interested in keeping relationships with the vendors and suppliers that sell goods or services to your company. They will spend time in this area in order to determine risks. They will want to know if their costs will go higher if they purchase your company and use the same vendors. They will look at many of your expenses, contracts, etc. in order to determine if there is any risk in this important area.

Contracts – Disclose all written contracts with key vendors and service providers. The buyer will want to know if there is an obligation to those contracts and/or if there are any risks associated with the contracts. The buyer will want to see if any vendors have security agreements against your company, such as a UCC filing on inventory or other assets. You will want to provide the most current UCC records from your county or local government. Care should be taken to go through the process to remove any UCC filings or liens that are recorded but no longer valid, such as a bank that filed a UCC on accounts receivable but the company is no longer doing business with that bank.

Foreign Vendors – It is not unusual for closely-held companies to purchase from foreign companies. These types of purchases sometimes require contracts and wire instructions and may include foreign currency transactional gains or losses. Disclose all material (significant) foreign currency transaction gains or losses during the past three years. These foreign vendors may or may not have any interest in doing business with the potential buyer and the buyer may view this as an area of significant risk, especially if your company is getting goods at a discount or with a certain quality necessary for your customers. Care should be given to carefully explain these foreign relationships to the prospective buyer.

Warranties – Certain products or services are purchased with warranties promised by vendors or service providers to your company. Provide all written documents that explain the warranty rights promised by vendors and service providers. Identify if any of these warranty rights are from foreign companies.

Related Parties – Closely-held companies often purchase goods or services from related parties (e.g., officers, directors, minority owners, immediate family members, affiliates, trusts, pensions and profit-sharing trusts). Disclose any such relationships to the potential buyer. Disclose situations in which the company pays a higher-than-market rate to these related parties for goods and services.

Key Vendors and Service Providers
Checklist

#	Subject	Description	n/a	Assigned To	Expected Completion Date	Completed & in the Data Room
1	Top 10	List the top 10 vendors and service providers during the past three years				
2	Contracts	Copies of all contracts, including any joint venture agreements with current or pending vendors and service providers				
3	Consign	Describe any purchases that are on consignment from the vendor				
4	Foreign	List all vendors and service providers that are foreign companies. Include any past foreign currency transaction losses or gains				
5	Declines	Describe any vendors and service providers that have refused to do business with the company				
6	Discounts, Pricing	List discounts, markdowns or special pricing arrangements with key vendors and service providers				
7	Lapsing Discounts	List all significant discounts, markdowns or special arrangements with key vendors or service providers that are about to terminate or lapse in the near future				
8	Warranties	List all product or service warranties and guarantees made to the company by key vendors and service providers				
9	Related Parties	List any key vendors and service providers that are related parties (e.g., immediate family members, investors, employees, officers)				

Key Vendors and Service Providers
Checklist
(continued)

#	Subject	Description	n/a	Assigned To	Expected Completion Date	Completed & in the Data Room
10	Security Agreements	List any security agreements, including recent UCC records, from any key vendors or service providers that have a lien on any company assets, including inventory				
11	Financing, Credit	Describe and list any financing (credit) terms by key vendors and service providers				
12	Discounts	List any discount offers or agreements by key vendors and service providers				
13	Backlog	A detail of backlog of materials or services from key vendors or service providers				
14	Financial Trouble	Detail any key vendors or service providers that you feel or know is having financial difficulty				

Chapter 14

Intellectual Property and Intangible Assets Checklist

Comment – The subject of intellectual property and intangible assets may be one of the key reasons a buyer decides to either purchase your company or that of a competitor. This is a complex subject, and ownership of intellectual property may be subject to interpretation or litigation. *The Success Team*™ should consult with attorneys who specialize in this area to make sure the assets your company claims to own are protected.

One of the specific factors in the valuation of your business is whether you have legally protected intellectual property assets, such as patents, trademarks and copyrights. Your intellectual property assets will assist the buyer in protecting the business from competition and, therefore, makes the business more attractive to the buyer.

Most business people do not know that they even have intellectual property assets to protect. For example, even if you have a nontechnology business, you may still be able to obtain a business method patent on some process or methodology that you use in conducting your business. Likewise, you may have trademarks, service marks, and trade dress that you use in your business that should be legally protected.

Long before your sale target date you should hire a patent or intellectual property attorney to help you identify your intellectual property assets. The process of obtaining patents can take three or four years; it is never too early to begin such a review. [70]

Trade Secrets – Trade secrets are very different from copyright ownership. These trade secrets may be the "secret sauce" to your company's processes, sales or other reasons for success. Trade secrets often may not be documented in a way that can currently be communicated to a prospective buyer. Your company wants to disclose trade secrets only upon close scrutiny and advice from attorneys who specialize in this subject matter. There may be significant risks or rewards with your company's trade secrets. The risk may be in disclosing this information in an improper manner to a prospective buyer, especially if that prospective buyer is a competitor. The reward may be a significant financial or negotiating tool if this information is indeed a "secret sauce" and if it is disclosed in the proper manner to the prospective buyer.

Trademarks – These assets are usually governed by the United States Patent and Trademark Office (USPTO). Their rules are complex and often seem arbitrary. They are presently overburdened with applications and processing, and they may work slower than you are accustomed to when requesting assistance. Your company will want to disclose all trademarks owned, including the registration number related to the trademark as issued by the USPTO. A list should be compiled of all trademarks that are in the process of approval and any trademarks that are used but are not owned by the company. This list should include trademarks and applications by subsidiary companies.

Patents – The patents owned by your company and/or a subsidiary may be worth significant amounts of money. List all patents issued by the USPTO, including abandoned applications and invention disclosures. Include this information for both domestic and foreign patents.

Third Parties – Companies sometimes license intellectual property from third parties. This licensing process is typically in the form of a contract or a series of contracts. This intellectual property may be important to the buyer in the consideration of the purchase. Disclose any and all licensing contracts to the prospective buyer after consultation with the attorney on *The Success Team*™. The buyer will want to know whether these licenses are transferable and the future estimated costs of using these licenses.

Intellectual Property and Intangible Assets
Checklist

#	Subject	Description	n/a	Assigned To	Expected Completion Date	Completed & in the Data Room
1	Trade-marks	All trademarks, including registration numbers. Include any important unregistered trademarks used by the company				
2	Patents	All issued patents, patent applications, abandoned applications and invention disclosures. Include all such items for both domestic and foreign patents				
3	Copyrights	All copyright registrations and important unregistered copyrights				
4	Service Marks	All service marks, including any important unregistered service marks				
5	Third-Party Intellectual Property	A complete list and copies of all agreements with third parties involving intellectual property assets. Describe the owner-business arrangement between the company and the owner				
6	Litigation or Claims	Any litigation and/or claims by or against the company about any intellectual property, whether owned by the company				
7	Royalties	Describe any royalties paid or received in intellectual property and whether such assets were jointly developed by others				
8	Trade Secrets	Describe the principal processes and other proprietary information considered by the company to be trade secrets, including copies of written company policies and procedures regarding the protection of these trade secrets				

Intellectual Property and Intangible Assets
Checklist
(continued)

#	Subject	Description	n/a	Assigned To	Expected Completion Date	Completed & in the Data Room
9	In Progress	Describe new principle processes the company is in the process of developing				
10	Employees	Describe any written or verbal agreements with sharing ownership or revenue with any company employee, both past and current employees				
11	Goodwill	Schedule of any goodwill owned				
12	Intangibles	Schedule of intangible assets (e.g., customer lists, research & development, search engine optimization)				

Chapter 15

Technology, Software and Hardware Checklist

Website – Websites of many closely-held companies are often some of their major assets. Your company's website should be on the list of assets owned. It is not uncommon for companies to own multiple websites and/or intranet sites, all of which may be of value to the buyer. It may be in your company's best interest to write a detailed description of how your website separates your company from its competition. Include any intranet used by employees, customers or vendors.

Webmaster – The webmaster of your company's website is a key factor in the sale of the company. Webmasters can hold a buy-sell transaction "hostage" and can unilaterally cause the transaction not to close. Some companies use an off-site, one-man-shop subcontractor, which the buyer will view as a significant risk. These types of subcontractors rarely have redundant backup plans. They typically do not have much documentation about source codes, the software used for the website, purchases of licenses, etc. They normally have numerous passwords and usernames, and have control over all of those in the company who use passwords and usernames. Webmasters who are employees need to give management detailed information about the website, where it is hosted, the source code, the software used for the websites, the license numbers — both those that are current and those that are expired — the usernames and passwords for everyone in the company, etc. The buyer will want to see the contract with any third-party webmaster and may want to do an on-site visit to the webmaster's place of business. Some webmasters are, by nature, skeptical of anyone who wants documentation or control of the website information. The company may want to hire a third-party vendor to verify all information about the website. This information should also include the company's Disaster Recovery Plan (DRP) in the case of a crash of the website and the information contained therein.

Software – Your company wants to immediately begin the process of documenting all of the software used by everyone in the company, software that is used both on-site and off-site. It will also include software that is used to run both the on-site and off-site file servers. The list should then be compared to the licenses purchased for each of the company's software applications. Companies are sometimes surprised by the number of software applications used that do not have legally purchased licenses. Unlicensed software should be immediately brought to the attention of *The Success Team*™. Not only is the use of unlicensed software illegal, there are financial incentives that can be awarded to current and past employees who "blow the whistle" on the company for using unlicensed software. Often, this unlicensed software is used without the knowledge of management. Unfortunately, ignorance of the usage of unlicensed software is not a defense and lawsuits can be filed against the company, the owners and management. The buyer will view this subject matter as a significant risk. It is best to get ahead of the buyer and provide adequate documentation, not only about the proper usage of licensed software but also about projected dates of when licenses might expire.

Proprietary Software – Some companies have created their own software to run the business. This software may or may not have legal protection and should be discussed with the members of *The Success Team*™ before presentation of the software to the prospective buyer. This software may become a key asset in the buy-sell transaction. This software would include any that is currently being programmed by the company for a future release.

Technology, Software and Hardware
Checklist

#	Subject	Description	n/a	Assigned To	Expected Completion Date	Completed & in the Data Room
1	Website and Intranet	List all websites used and/or owned by the company. Include all URLs and the owner of the URLs. Include any intranet used by employees, customers or vendors. Detail of where this software is hosted				
2	Webmaster	List the name and location of the webmaster and whether this is an employee or subcontractor relationship				
3	DRP	Describe the company's Disaster Recovery Program (DRP) for all data and software				
4	SEO	List keywords and meta tags and processes used for all Search Engine Optimization				
5	SEM	List all keywords and processes used for the company's Search Engine Marketing				
6	Software	Schedule of all material software, databases and systems owned, developed or licensed by the company. Include maintenance agreements and lapsing dates				
7	Licenses	List of all licenses for all software used by the company, including the license number, software company and lapsing dates				
8	Planned Software	Schedule of all material ongoing or planned software, database or network development projects. Include budgets for the current and next fiscal year				
9	Cloud	List of all cloud-based software used or where data is stored, including licenses, user names and passwords				

Technology, Software and Hardware
Checklist
(continued)

#	Subject	Description	n/a	Assigned To	Expected Completion Date	Completed & in the Data Room
10	Software Owned	List all software developed by the company and/or a related party. List all copyrights or restrictions on the software				
11	Hardware	List all computer hardware used by the company, whether on-site or off-site. Detail the names of those that maintain the hardware. Detail any liens on the equipment by bankers, lenders, leasing companies, etc.				
12	Restrictions	Identify any restrictions on the transfer or change of control of software. Explain any conflicts that might arise related to the use of the software				

branding

Chapter 16

Branding, Marketing and Public Relations Checklist

Branding – The subject of branding and selling a business is an interesting topic. In layman's terms, branding is the process of using techniques to grow the business by separating one's company from the competition in a demonstrable and strategic manner. Realizing that most sales transactions fail, one could argue that a business owner should continually try to improve upon the company's brand.
Otherwise, a company runs the risk of failing to be distinguished from the competition, which eventually might erode sales and the overall value of the company. This might, in turn, hurt the ability for a future sale to a future buyer.

A buyer may or may not be interested in your company's brand. For example, a strategic buyer, such as a larger competitor, may be interested in buying your customers, processes, employees and other assets in order to gain a larger market share. The buyer may want to roll your company into theirs and completely drop your branding. This makes sense if it meets the needs of the buyer.

A financial buyer may be interested in keeping the brand name. For example, in 2002 a company named Zappos.com had sales of $32M but was not yet profitable. Tony Hsieh, the CEO, made a bold move and decided to change the brand of the company to "customer service." He stated,

We realized the biggest vision would be **to build the Zappos brand** *to be about the very best customer service.*[71]

The branding solution worked. The company grew tremendously and was sold to Amazon in 2009. As of the time of the writing of this book, the Zappos.com website does not show the name or the brand of the buyer, Amazon. This was clearly a financial purchase by Amazon, which decided that the existing branding of Zappos was important enough to keep the Zappos name instead of rolling it into the Amazon name.

Public Relations – Press releases and other such processes are important to the growth and branding efforts of some companies. For example, our company did not have one press release prior to 2007. We hired a public relations firm, Angles Public Relations, and we slowly began to receive press coverage. Today, we have so much press coverage that we have found it necessary to build an entire website (www.news.b2bcfo.com) just to hold all of the press releases, television appearances, etc. It may be coincidental, but our company has grown more than 400% over the period of time we have been using public relations.

Buyers will want to see your past press clippings and published news articles. They will also want to know if your company has a future public relations plan.

Branding, Marketing and Public Relations
Checklist

#	Subject	Description	n/a	Assigned To	Expected Completion Date	Completed & in the Data Room
1	Plan	Describe the company's branding, marketing and public relations plan				
2	Inside	Provide the resumes and job descriptions of any internal graphic artists, marketing, branding and public relations employees				
3	Outside	List the names, addresses and a description of the outside subcontractors used in graphic arts, marketing, branding and public relations				
4	Printed Material	Provide all brochures, literature, forms, catalogs and other material issued to the public and otherwise used in marketing, branding and public relations				
5	Website	Provide any website names and URLs used for or by the company in its marketing, branding and public relations				
6	Trademarks	Provide the trademark names for all trademarks owned or used by the company including the registration number issued by the United States Patent and Trademark Office				
7	Applications	Provide the trademark names for all trademarks applied for, including current printouts of registration status by the United States Patent and Trademark Office				
8	Non-Owned	Detail any trademarks used (e.g., brochures, websites, any printed material) that are not owned by the company				
9	Disaster Plan	Provide a copy of the company's disaster plan in the event of a highly negative public relations issue				

Branding, Marketing and Public Relations
Checklist
(continued)

#	Subject	Description	n/a	Assigned To	Expected Completion Date	Completed & in the Data Room
10	Reports	List and copy of all marketing and public relations reports prepared for management. Indicate which are done on a daily, weekly, monthly or annual basis				
11	Articles, Press Releases	Copies of all articles and press releases about the company and its officers for the past three years				
12	Foreign	List all foreign branding, marketing and public relations work during the past three years				

Chapter 17

Related Parties and Minority Owners Checklist

Minority Owners – Minority owners may be your best friend or your worst nightmare during a sales transaction. Success with these people depends much on the documentation of their ownership, the nature of your current relationship and their future goals. Much also depends upon the amount of money they want from the sales transaction and whether they feel they are being treated fairly with the proceeds from the impending sale.

Existing minority owners typically fall into two categories (1) they are friendly and helpful or (2) they are angry and can become hostile. It is the latter that becomes the problem during the sales transaction. This sensitive matter may need to be discussed with your attorney and *The Success Team*™ to create a plan of action. Full disclosure is critical with minority owners in an impending sales transaction.

> *Make full disclosure in writing to the minority equityholder of any favorable facts or trends that would be material to a selling minority equityholder before the minority equityholder becomes legally obligated to complete the sale. This is not only a best practice, but may be legally required by federal and state securities laws, as well as by fiduciary-duty standards, whether or not the sale is initiated by the minority equityholder.* [72]

Owners are sometimes tempted to give out ownership of the company with the event of a future or impending sale. Their logic is that they need these people to sell the company and to have an incentive to possibly stay with the company if they are viewed as important to the prospective buyer. The following advice has previously been written in this book:

> *Don't issue stock options to retain key employees after an acquisition. Instead, use a simple stay bonus that offers the members of your management team a cash reward if you sell your company. Pay the reward in two or three installments only to those who stay so that you can ensure your key staff stays on through the transition.* [73]

Family Members – Many closely-held companies have family members who work for the company. These people are often very loyal and hardworking. Some family members are the opposite. Some are paid at or below their market price, with market price being defined as the cost of replacing them with a nonfamily member. Some family members receive salaries and other perks that are significantly above market price.

The buyer needs to know about all family members and related party transactions. They need to know what positions they hold and their entire compensation. The buyer may or may not decide to keep these family members as employees after the transaction closes.

Related Parties – Many closely-held companies have business dealings with related parties, which can be defined to include officers, directors, minority owners, immediate family members, affiliates, etc. The buyer will want to know all contracts (written and oral) and to know all business relationships with them, especially if a relationship is troubled or about to go into litigation

Related Parties and Minority Owners
Checklist

#	Subject	Description	n/a	Assigned To	Expected Completion Date	Completed & in the Data Room
1	Minority Owners	List all minority owner names and the percentages owned of the company				
2	Ownership	List any minority owner interests by the company in other entities or affiliates				
3	Related Parties	List all related parties that have current and past transactions with the company (e.g., officers, directors, minority owners, immediate family members, affiliates, trusts, pensions and profit-sharing trusts)				
4	Employees	List of all employees and subcontractors who are immediate family members				
5	Contracts	Copy or describe all contracts or agreements (written or oral) with related parties or minority owners of any kind (e.g., partnerships, joint ventures, service agreements, insurance, leasing, consulting, cost-sharing, management agreements)				
6	Troubled Relationship	Describe any troubled relationship of any kind with a related party or minority owner, and describe management's desired result with this troubled relationship (e.g., purchase minority owner or family member interests, litigation, arbitration, negotiation)				

Related Parties and Minority Owners
Checklist
(continued)

#	Subject	Description	n/a	Assigned To	Expected Completion Date	Completed & in the Data Room
7	Assets	List any off-site assets owned by the company but that are in the possession of minority owners or related parties (e.g., automobiles, houses, equipment, computer hardware and software, customer lists, intellectual property, trade secrets)				
8	Benefits	List all benefits provided to related parties and minority owners, even if the person is not officially employed by the company (e.g., health insurance, retirement benefits, automobiles, computers)				
9	Transactions	Document any large, unusual, or nonrecurring transactions or balances, including loans receivable or loans payable with related parties or minority owners				

Chapter 18

Insurance Checklist

Key Man Insurance - This subject is often at the bottom of the list of things to do for a business owner who is contemplating the sale of a business. Understood properly, this topic should really be at the top of the list and should be in place before the sales transaction process begins.

Why are you thinking about selling your company? There may be many reasons but you will not be able to sell the company unless it has one key ingredient: **Value to a buyer**.

That value is important to a lot of people in the event that you prematurely die before the sales transaction closes. An untimely death that is not adequately covered by key man insurance can cause significant problems for the estate and/or minority shareholders of the deceased business owner. There are, after all, obligations that might continue long after your death, and it is your responsibility to make sure those items are planned for and adequately insured. Some that might have an interest in your company due to an untimely death might be:

- **The Internal Revenue Service** – The estate tax rates are very high and they can take much money from your estate, as is illustrated in the stories about the Miami Dolphins and Chicago Cubs, below.

- **Bankers, Lenders and Creditors** – They will want to be paid in full for the debts owed by the company. Some assets of the company may not be liquid or may not cover the full amounts owed, and the company might require insurance to pay debts.

- **Litigants** – There may be lawsuits filed against your company subsequent to your premature death.

- **Business Continuity** – Your current employees, family members and others may want a job and may want to continue with the company subsequent to your premature death.

The Internal Revenue Service (IRS) is desperate for cash. Our federal government's annual cash burn-rate exceeds its annual cash intake. The IRS is keenly interested in the value of your company, whether you are dead or alive. They expect to extract every farthing of taxes they can legally take. Below are a couple of famous cases regarding the IRS and business owners who did not have adequate key man life insurance to cover the estate taxes owed after their death.

> *Joseph "Joe" Robbie was the original owner of the NFL football team, the Miami Dolphins (1966-1990). Coached by Don Shula, Robbie's Dolphins achieved a perfect season (17-0) in 1972 and two consecutive Super Bowl wins.* [74]

> *When Joe Robbie passed away in 1990, his family had to sell the franchise (in 1994) to pay a reported $47 million in estate taxes.* [75]

> *Robbie's estate was somewhat less than $100 million and almost 50% of it vanished in federal estate taxes. It compelled his family to sell the Dolphins at a fraction of its value. Strife and bitter resentments developed within the family because of the actions they had to take to pay the taxes. The real tragedy is that it all could have been avoided.*

If that $45 million could have been **paid with a life insurance check,** *concluded Financial Planning (magazine),* **it would have certainly changed the financial complexion of the family's situation.** [76]

A similar situation happened to the Wrigley family and the Chicago Cubs:

> *The Wrigley family had to sell the Chicago Cubs to pay taxes that came due upon the death of two members of the family.* [77]

The moral of this story is to make sure you have adequate insurance in the event of a premature death.

Insurance Beneficiaries – The insurance advisor will want to audit and report the beneficiaries of all life insurance policies to *The Success Team™*. The team will want to discuss the beneficiaries with you and give you advice. It is unwise to assume that you know the beneficiaries of each insurance policy who have been recorded on the records of the insurance company.

One of the partners in B2B CFO® was hired by a company about two weeks after Rick, the former CEO, was brutally murdered. Paris, the new CEO, was hired to run the company a few days after the murder. The new CEO was told by the former CEO that he had purchased $5 million in a key man life insurance policy to pay creditors in full and to have the company continue in business should he experience a premature death. Below is a shocking account about the issue of named beneficiaries and key man life insurance.

> *He (Paris) knew that Rick had a very large seven-figure life insurance policy ($5 million) that was to go to the company in order to help it survive. The life insurance policy was apparently changed prior to Rick's death, and the beneficiary was changed to have the life insurance proceeds go to a family member, rather than to the designated trust (which owned the stock of the company). The estate professionals and others who had created and/or had seen Rick's legal will were shocked to see the money go to the family member. Nobody really seemed to know who had changed the beneficiary name on the life insurance papers, but several felt the name had been changed against Rick's desires.* [78]

The new CEO never received the $5 million to pay the creditors and to continue the business. Eventually, the company filed Chapter 11 bankruptcy and the company was sold at a fire-sale price to the creditors.

Insurance
Checklist

#	Subject	Description	n/a	Assigned To	Expected Completion Date	Completed & in the Data Room
1	Current Policies	Detail of insurance policies (e.g., product liability, property & casualty, general liability, errors & omissions, directors & officers, disability, key-man life, employee disability, travel & accident, business interruption, automobile, employee bonds, shipping, umbrella, workers' compensation)				
2	Claims	Detail of the claims on insurance for the past five years and any pending claims on insurance policies (e.g., product liability, property & casualty, general liability, errors & omissions, directors & officers, disability, key-man life, employee disability, travel & accident, business interruption, automobile, employee bonds, shipping, umbrella, workers' compensation)				
3	Self Insurance	Detail of self/captive insurance policies and programs, history of claims, etc. Describe in detail why the company decided to use self insurance				
4	Not Covered	Describe any liability of the company, its officers or employees that is not covered by adequate insurance				
5	Buy/Sell Agreements	Copy of any buy-sell agreement entered into by the company and the insurance that supports this document				
6	Key-Man	Describe the key-man life insurance policy and whether the policy is adequate				
7	Agents	The names and contact information of all agents and brokers for all insurance policies				

Insurance
Checklist
(continued)

#	Subject	Description	n/a	Assigned To	Expected Completion Date	Completed & in the Data Room
8	Guarantees	Describe all insurance policies that are used to guarantee loan or mortgage agreements				
9	Rejection	Detail of any important insurance policies applied for by the company that have been rejected by insurance companies during the past three years				

Chapter 19

Internal Financial Information Checklist

Overview – Your business acumen will be judged severely by a prospective buyer regarding the information in this chapter. Having bad internal financial information is the fastest method you can use to chase away a good prospective buyer. The buyer will expect information to be accurate and in accordance with Generally Accepted Accounting Principles (GAAP). The buyer will expect your monthly records to be closed on a timely basis, by around the 10th to 15th day of the following month. Everything you do is either enhanced or made suspect by the timeliness and accuracy of your company's internal financial information.

> *The lack of financial integrity is one of the most common hurdles encountered during the sales process.*

> *The owner of (the) business tells (the buyer) that the company has been making $5 million per year for the past three years and expects it to make even more in the future. Are you really surprised that the buyer's first thought is, "Prove it!"? If a seller then produces financial information that proves incorrect, insupportable or incomplete, the buyer will be highly skeptical or, more likely, simply gone. You would never pay millions of dollars without complete confidence in the company's financial information. Should your buyer?* [79]

Balance Sheet Errors – It has been our experience that almost all companies have material errors on their balance sheets. These errors are often compounded if the company owns subsidiary companies. It is critical to fix any potential errors on the balance sheets prior to showing them to a prospective buyer. Procedures should then be established to help minimize the future likelihood of such errors being recorded on your company's balance sheets. Common errors on balance sheets include such items as:

- Cash that has not been reconciled correctly
- Inventory, such as obsolete items or errors in the computer
- Accounts receivables that should be written off to bad debt expense
- Recording depreciation on the tax basis instead of the GAAP basis
- Expensing prepaid items instead of capitalizing them
- Accounts payable amounts either unrecorded or recorded in the wrong period
- Errors in accruals, such as accrued payroll
- Long-term debt that does not agree with loan amortization tables
- Errors in Owner's Equity
- Etc.

Revenue Recognition – The revenue recognition policy of the company will be looked at very closely. The buyer will look at the matching of revenue and expenses to determine if they feel the financial statements are properly stated.

> *If you recognize yourself as an owner who has been overly aggressive in shifting income and expenses, (or, more likely, have given the financial controls insufficient attention over the years) it is of fundamental importance to the entire sale process that your past aggressiveness be diligently reviewed and corrected where appropriate.* [80]

Projections – One of the most important parts of making projections about future income and expenses is the documentation of the key assumptions used. This is the area where companies usually fail in making projections. The buyer will scrutinize the assumptions and ask for a lot of detail about how your staff arrived at the conclusions of the assumptions. They will want to see backup and proof of all key assumptions. Additionally, errors on the balance sheets, described above, will often cause errors on projections about future income and expenses.

Internal Financial Information
Checklist

#	Subject	Description	n/a	Assigned To	Expected Completion Date	Completed & in the Data Room
1	Historical	Balance Sheets, Income Statements and Statements of Cash Flow - past three years				
2	Current	Balance Sheets, Income Statements and Statements of Cash Flow – most current				
3	Projections	Projections of Income Statements and Balance Sheets for the next three years, including a detail of key assumptions and potential risks to the projections				
4	Revenue Recognition	The Revenue Recognition policy of the company (e.g., Percentage of Completion, Accrual Basis, Cash Basis, Deferred Income)				
5	Accounts Receivable	The most recent accounts receivable aging; identify bad debts and describe the company's policy to determine bad debts				
6	Notes Receivable	Copies of all notes receivables due from customers, employees, etc.				
7	Fixed Assets	A detailed list of fixed assets, including location and the depreciation policy. List all obsolete or damaged assets.				
8	Accounts Payable	The most recent accounts payable aging. Explain material amounts owed 60+ days				
9	Accruals	List of material accruals				
10	Notes Payable and Lines of Credit	Debt Summary, including debt to related parties. List the terms (e.g., interest rate, balloon payments, number of months owed on the note, guarantees, loans in default cross-collateralization)				
11	Leases	Copies of all material leases				

Internal Financial Information
Checklist
(continued)

#	Subject	Description	n/a	Assigned To	Expected Completion Date	Completed & in the Data Room
12	Contingent Liabilities	List all contingent liabilities of the company (e.g., liabilities that may be incurred by an entity depending on the outcome of a future event such as litigation, regulatory change, negotiations)				
13	Business Plan	Copy of any business plan presented to bankers, lenders, investors or third parties during the past three years				
14	Capital Budget	List all material capital expenditures the company needs to make to accomplish future projected growth				

Chapter 20

Inventory Checklist

Overview – Many companies have inventory. Inventory is often fraught with potential problems. The errors listed below may increase or decrease inventory on the Balance Sheet. These increases or decreases will directly impact your company's Income Statement:

- Obsolete items that have a value lower than cost
- Negative quantities in the inventory printout
- Quantity errors on the inventory printout
- Errors in the recorded cost of inventory
- Inventory shipped to a customer but not deducted from inventory
- Inventory received from a vendor but not yet recorded into inventory
- Incorrect part numbers
- Theft of inventory that has not been recorded
- Theft of inventory by employees that is covered up by other inventory errors
- Consignment inventory issues
- Etc.

BTPA – The buyers will be interested in the details and the amount of the company's Book-to-Physical-Adjustments (BTPA) for the past few years. They will study this information to see if they agree with the assumptions made on the adjustments. They will want to see the inventory policies and procedures of the company regarding the inventory counts, controls, etc. They will expect to see tight internal controls on the cutoff of inventory receipts and the corresponding policies on shipments. These are seasoned veterans about inventory, and they will attempt to find any weakness possible in your inventory amount and the related controls.

Work-In-Progress (WIP) – Companies that recognize revenue on a percentage of completion, work-in-progress or in a manufacturing environment can expect to provide much detail on their inventory. Buyers will want to see details on your WIP as well as how materials and labor are reported in the inventory, both with direct and indirect expenditures. They will want to look at the detail for Uniform Capitalization Rules (UNICAP) for companies that are in manufacturing or that would otherwise fall into UNICAP, a tax concept governed by United States Internal Revenue Code.

Increases in Costs – Some companies have unexpected increases in inventory costs, both for material and labor. Documentation should be made and shared with the buyer if any of these costs are viewed by your company as unusual and that might be expected to be lower in the future. For example, perhaps foreign goods were purchased at unusually high costs due to unusual fluctuations in foreign currency transactions, due to unusual situations, such as an act of God, a terrorist attack, a strike or something else. It might be appropriate to share this information with a prospective buyer, assuming the foreign currency lowered to a normal level after a period of time.

As a rule of thumb, your company should look at its own inventory as if it had to write a check to purchase the entire inventory. What measures would you and your management take to make sure the amount paid for the inventory would be realized at your company's expected margins when sold to its customers?

Inventory
Checklist

#	Subject	Description	n/a	Assigned To	Expected Completion Date	Completed & in the Data Room
1	Inventory	Print a detail of the most current inventory				
2	Obsolete	Identify any obsolete inventory and the projected amount and write-down date of the obsolete inventory				
3	Turnover	List the inventory turnover rates				
4	Not Available	List any important inventory that is not or soon will not be available to be purchased				
5	Gross Profit Analysis	Provide an overall gross profit analysis for the past three years. Provide a gross profit analysis for inventory that constitutes a material percentage of cost of goods sold				
6	BTPA	Give the date of the last physical inventory count. List the amount and describe the reason(s) for any material book-to-physical adjustment (BTPA)				
7	Projection	A report on the projected inventory usage for the next 12 months				
8	Valuation	A description of the company's policy for valuing inventory, including labor, outside materials and overhead				
9	Negative Quantities	Identify any negative quantities in the most current inventory list and the company's policy to fix such items in the future				
10	Software	Describe the company's software used for the inventory. List the owner of the software, the license number and the expiration date of the license				
11	Concerns	Describe any concerns management has about the company's inventory (e.g., labor, valuation, pressure from any competitors – including foreign competition, current or future governmental regulations)				

Inventory
Checklist
(continued)

#	Subject	Description	n/a	Assigned To	Expected Completion Date	Completed & in the Data Room
12	Shrinkage	Describe material inventory shrinkage during the past three years (e.g., inventory that was stolen, disappeared) and management's policies to resolve the issue				
13	Vendors	A list of the vendors that provide inventory				
14	Discounts	Any arrangements that allow the company to buy inventory at a discount not available to most of the company's competition				

Chapter 21

External Financial Statements Checklist

Overview – It is unusual to go through a sales transaction without examined financial statements from independent CPAs for the past several years. There are exceptions to this rule — companies that are unique, situations where there are multiple buyers, etc.

> *As a general rule, a company with less than $5M in Adjusted EBITDA might be able to sell the company with reviewed financial statements by an independent CPA firm. Any company with more than $5M in Adjusted EBITDA that does not have audited financial statements will raise red flags.*
>
> *Larry Reinharz, Managing Director, Woodbridge International*

The Business Reason – Buyers take risks when they purchase companies. They are sophisticated enough to know that financial statements examined by an independent CPA firm, while not error proof, give them the best opportunity to rely upon the financial information provided by a privately-held company. In addition to the audit or review report, they especially look at disclosures that are in the financial statements. The examined statements may have as many as 12 to 20 pages of disclosed information about your company.

The examined financial statements also give buyers an important tool. They use these statements to compare to the selling company's past internal financial statements. They do this in order to see if there are significant differences between the internal financial statements and the examined statements. This information is then used to judge the credibility of the internal financial statements for periods of time they look at that may not be examined by the CPA firm.

> *An audited financial statement provides the buyer with a greater assurance of your financial results.*
>
> Frederick D. Lipman [81]

> *The best way to document the company (1) has effective financial controls and (2) its historical financial statements are correct is through a certified audit by an established CPA firm.*
>
> John H. Brown [82]

Experience – Financial examinations, especially audits by independent CPAs, are a difficult and time-consuming process. The degree of difficulty in this process increases if a company has never previously had a financial examination. It is in your best interest to have a person who works internally who has either worked for a CPA firm in an audit capacity or who has worked at a company that had CPA examinations and knows how to work with them. This person can assist with communication, help with sensitive matters uncovered by the CPA firm, work with the staff to try to minimize their time spent on providing information, assist to streamline the process, etc.

The Gamble – Unless your company has previously been examined, one of the most difficult decisions you and *The Success Team*™ will make during the exit strategy process is if your company will hire and pay for the independent CPA firm's examination or if this will be done by the buyer. Below are some things to consider with either decision you make.

THE BUYER HIRES THE INDEPENDENT AUDITORS

The Buyer Hires – There are advantages and disadvantages to your company if the buyer hires the CPA firm to perform the examination.

> *Audits can wreak havoc on a deal for two reasons. First, if not properly prepared for, they can add two to four months to the length of the deal. Secondly, **audits provide buyers with a host of reasons to lower the price**.*
>
> *John H. Brown* [83]

Advantage or Disadvantage	Reason
Advantage	The buyer pays the cost of the audit, which can sometimes be a six-figure amount (Some feel this cost is eventually transferred to the seller, but this is subject to opinion.).
Disadvantage	The buyer will hire the CPA firm, sometimes without any input from your company. Auditors are supposed to be independent and, hopefully, they will not be the CPA firm that also examines the buyer and/or one or more of their subsidiary companies.

THE BUYER HIRES THE INDEPENDENT AUDITORS
(continued)

Advantage or Disadvantage	Reason
Disadvantage	The auditors may report irregularities (whether real or assumed) to the buyer before they are reported to your company.
Disadvantage	The time frame of the examination may be condensed, perhaps to just a few months. This short period may not give your company time to fix irregularities or to provide proof that things are different from the assumptions made by the CPA firm.
Disadvantage	The CPA firm will consume much of your accounting staff's time during the examination period. The staff may be needed to do other things during this period of time, such as work on the operations of the company, work on the numerous other tasks contained in the checklists in this book, perform their normal day-to-day duties, etc.
Disadvantage	The CPA firm may simultaneously do three or more years of examinations if your company has never had an examination performed by an independent CPA firm.

THE SELLER HIRES THE INDEPENDENT AUDITORS

Your company hires – There are advantages and disadvantages if your company hires the CPA firm to perform the examination.

Advantage or Disadvantage	Reason
Disadvantage	Your company will pay the cost of the examination, which can sometimes be a six-figure amount if the period of time is three years or more.
Advantage	The examination might be performed over a longer period of time, perhaps 18 to 24 months. This will allow your company to spread the cost over a longer period of time. This will also give your staff some breathing room and valuable time to fix any important irregularities or procedures found by the CPAs, hopefully before they issue the examination report.
Advantage	*The Success Team*™ and you might be able to find a CPA firm that is a known entity and that has developed good relationships with members of the team. You might also find someone who works well with your tax CPA and other professionals to open important communication channels that might be needed during the course of the examination.

THE SELLER HIRES THE INDEPENDENT AUDITORS
(continued)

Advantage or Disadvantage	Reason
Advantage	Given adequate time, a CPA firm may be able to put the examination on hold to give your company time to improve upon important procedures, fix irregularities, find important documentation, etc. This period of time may be used to not only fix the issues raised by the CPA firm but may eventually add more value to the sales price of the company.
Advantage	The examination may be done one year at a time instead of several years at a time.
Advantage	An experienced internal person, discussed above, may be able to have the staff complete PBCs (documents prepared by the client), write drafts of footnotes, and do other tasks with the goal of lowering the examination fees charged by the independent CPA firm.

External Financial Statements
Checklist

#	Subject	Description	n/a	Assigned To	Expected Completion Date	Completed & in the Data Room
1	Audits	Copies of all audits by independent Certified Public Accountants (CPAs) for the past three years, including the auditor's report				
2	Other Reports	Copies of any reports of any kind from independent CPAs for the past three years (projections, appraisals, etc.)				
3	Incomplete Reports	All correspondence from independent CPAs and/or attorneys regarding audits, reviews, compilations or other projects of which the CPAs were not able to complete the work contracted for in the Engagement Letters for the past five years				
4	Engagement Letters	Copies of all Engagement Letters from independent CPAs for the past five years				
5	Related Parties or Subsidiaries	Copies of audits, tax returns or other material prepared by independent CPAs for any of the company's related parties and/or subsidiaries for the past three years				
6	Names & Addresses	Names and addresses of all parties that have performed any external financial statement engagements for the company for the past five years				

Chapter 22

Contracts and Leases Checklist

Overview – We have not previously written about this subject in this book. The topic of this chapter is an opportunity to bring this important information to your attention.

The buyer has a couple of options in purchasing your company. The buyer can either purchase the company's stock or its assets. These are two entirely different transactions. Both of these transactions might cause different risks to both the buyer and the seller. They also have different income tax treatment to both parties. This chapter is not a comprehensive discussion of this subject matter, but this may be a good starting point for you and *The Success Team*™.

Stock Purchase – The buyer may offer to purchase the stock of the company, or the membership interest if the company is a limited liability company (LLC). This type of purchase presents interesting risks to the buyer. The buyer is the owner of 100% of the stock (or membership interests) after the close of the transaction. The buyer then receives the benefit of the cash, revenue and other assets of the company. The buyer also is at risk for the liabilities of the company, including certain contingent liabilities. These contingent liabilities might include unusually high warranty costs paid to past customers, lawsuits that are about to be filed, such as a sexual harassment lawsuit, a sales tax audit for the past several years that the buyer discovers after the transaction closes, a Department of Labor (DOL) audit claim that was recently filed by a disgruntled employee, etc. These and other reasons are why the buyer wants to see all contracts — loan documents, lease agreements, mortgage agreements, promissory notes, Uniform Commercial Code (UCC) filings, restrictions on competition, bond agreements, franchise agreements, etc.

A stock purchase might also cause interesting legal problems for the seller. It is not unusual for business owners, even minority owners, to give personal guarantees to notes, loans, leases, etc. The challenge to the seller then becomes receiving a complete release on all of these guarantees at the close of the transaction.

A seller sometimes pledges personal assets (e.g., personal residence, personal land, stock certificates, whole-life insurance policies) in order to obtain loans, leases, lines of credit and other financial instruments. The challenge to the seller becomes receiving a complete release on all personal assets pledged at the close of the transaction. The creditors may have no incentive to release the liens or UCC filings on your personal assets after you sell the stock in your company.

There are income tax implications to the seller of stock. These might include ordinary income, capital gains income, the loss of certain net operating loss carryforwards, deferred income taxes on net built-in gains from a prior change from a C-Corp to an S-Corp (this gain usually has a five- to 10-year life), taxes from the Affordable Health Care for America Act, etc. The company should have very good tax professionals (attorneys, CPAs) on The Success Team™ who can discuss these and other tax implications related to the sale of stock or LLC member interests.

Asset Purchase – An asset purchase of a closely-held company is the most commonly used purchase option. An asset purchase usually limits risks to the buyer, such as some of the contingent liabilities discussed above. An asset purchase can, however, open certain interesting risks to the buyer. For example, there may be UCC filings that have not been released on assets purchased, a factoring company might have checks from your customers sent to the factoring company instead of to your company, certain assets may have been cross-collateralized, etc. The buyer will want to review all contracts to look for anything that might impair any asset that has been purchased from the seller.

The seller in an asset purchase may have a larger income tax liability than with a sale of stock. The seller is usually responsible to pay off all or most of the debt of the company. The seller is also responsible for certain continuing liabilities, such as those discussed above (e.g., warranty costs paid to past customers, lawsuits that are about to be filed, such as a sexual harassment lawsuit, a sales tax audit for the past several years that the buyer finds out about after the transaction closes, a Department of Labor (DOL) audit claim that was recently filed by a disgruntled employee).

You may wish to have a discussion with attorneys and insurance advisors about the types of insurance policies you might need subsequent to the close of an asset purchase transaction. It may be wise to maintain certain policies, such as general liability, errors and omissions, etc.

Contracts and Leases
Checklist

#	Subject	Description	n/a	Assigned To	Expected Completion Date	Completed & in the Data Room
1	Debt Schedule	A schedule of outstanding debt of the company and any subsidiary or related party on any secured assets used by the company, including capitalized leases				
2	Leases	Copies of all lease agreements, including amortization tables for all capitalized leases				
3	Real Estate	Copies of all lease, loan or mortgage agreements on buildings. Include the locations of the real estate				
4	Equip-ment	All lease or loan agreements on equipment, furniture, fixtures, hardware or software				
5	Banks, Lenders & Investors	Copies of agreements with bank-ers, lenders and investors on lines of credit, promissory notes, and all loan or credit agreements				
6	Factoring	Any agreement to factor receivables or inventory of the company				
7	Guaran-tees	Disclose all guarantees of company loans by officers, family members or minority owners				
8	Bonding	Details of any bonding agreements or requirements				
9	Indemnify	Indemnification contracts or agreements by any officer, director, employee or related party against any liability incurred				
10	UCC	Copies of current UCC filings on the company, its subsidiaries or its related parties				
11	Restric-tions	Copies of contracts with any company or individual that restricts competition in any form or manner				
12	Franchise	Current or past franchise agreements, including any distributor agreements				

Contracts and Leases
Checklist
(continued)

#	Subject	Description	n/a	Assigned To	Expected Completion Date	Completed & in the Data Room
13	Marketing	Copies of all contracts with marketing, advertising or public relations companies				

Chapter 23

Litigation and Claims Checklist

Litigation – It is not unusual for closely-held companies to have lawsuits, either as the plaintiff, co-plaintiff, defendant or a co-defendant. The buyers will want to know everything they can about these lawsuits.

There may be confidential documents in the litigation papers that have been provided during interrogatories, depositions or requests for documents. No documentation should be provided to the buyer until the attorney who is handling the case allows disclosure and *The Success Team*™ has had an opportunity to discuss the matter.

Threatened Litigation – There is a balance between giving too much and too little information to a buyer about threatened litigation.

Too much information disclosed to the buyer may be used in discovery as evidence in the event the litigation occurs. Too little information can be viewed as an intentional lack of disclosure by the buyer. In either case, advice should be sought from attorneys and those on *The Success Team*™ related to threatened litigation.

Opinion Letter – Some buyers ask for legal opinion letters from the seller's attorney or law firm. They may ask for specific items, such as a lawsuit. They may ask for a general and broad-sweeping opinion about legal matters and risks related to your company.

Many owners have never seen such a letter and are unfamiliar with the issues and implications related to such a document.

Your company wants to be cautious before telling buyers that your attorney or law firm will give a legal opinion letter. Attorneys are sometimes reluctant to issue an opinion letter due to the risks involved with issuing the letter. Your company should not necessarily view an attorney negatively if the attorney refuses to issue an opinion letter about your company. The attorney simply may not have enough information and/or may feel the facts are in a developmental stage.

The opinion letter may cost your company a significant amount of money because of the time the law firm must spend in order to do its due diligence.

> *A "legal opinion" or "closing opinion," is a type of professional opinion, usually contained in a formal legal-opinion letter, given by an attorney to a client or a third party. Most legal opinions are given in connection with business transactions. The opinion expresses the attorney's professional judgment regarding the legal matters addressed. A legal opinion is not a guarantee that a court will reach any particular result. However, a mistaken or incomplete legal opinion may be grounds for a professional malpractice claim against the attorney, pursuant to which the attorney may be required to pay the claimant damages incurred as a result of relying on the faulty opinion.* [84]

Litigation and Claims
Checklist

#	Subject	Description	n/a	Assigned To	Expected Completion Date	Completed & in the Data Room
1	Plaintiff	List all lawsuits filed by the company as the plaintiff or co-plaintiff for the past five years, along with the results, the name and contact information of the company's law firm. Include parties involved, subject matter and amounts claimed				
2	Defendant	List all lawsuits filed against the company as a defendant or co-defendant for the past five years, along with the results, the name and contact information of the company's law firm. Include parties involved, subject matter and amounts claimed				
3	Threatened Litigation	A description of any threatened litigation or claims by the company as a plaintiff or defendant. Include parties involved, subject matter and amounts claimed				
4	Consents, Judgments, Settlements	Any decrees, orders and agreements to which the company is a party or is bound, requiring or prohibiting any future activities				
5	Government	Any material claims (or taxes) by any governmental regulatory authority: federal, state, local or any foreign country. Include parties involved, subject matter and amounts				
6	Arbitrations & Injunctions	A complete list of any arbitrations, injunctions and/or consent decrees on behalf or against the company for the past five years				

Litigation and Claims
Checklist
(continued)

#	Subject	Description	n/a	Assigned To	Expected Completion Date	Completed & in the Data Room
7	Risks	List of any significant legal risks against the company that might lead to possible litigation, arbitration, zoning or claims by any third party, current employee, past employee or governmental regulatory authority				
8	Criminal Charges	List any criminal charge, indictment, investigation or convictions of the company or its management				
9	Attorney Opinion Letters	Letters to the company by attorneys concerning the potential effects of any significant or pending changes in any state or federal law, rule or regulations				

Chapter 24

Taxes Checklist

Overview – We have deferred a sometimes uncomfortable discussion until this chapter.

We have hinted about this subject in an earlier chapter in this book.

> *Most closely held businesses are operated to minimize income taxes. As a result, excessive compensation and perquisites may be provided to the owner and his family in order to reduce taxes. The excessive compensation and perquisites are really forms of disguised dividends.* [85]

We have also disclosed in an earlier chapter the various ways that business owners can put personal expenses into the Income Statement of a company, such as:

- Personal legal costs for estate planning, divorce, personal litigation, etc.

- Tuition and educational expenses for children and family members
- Golf, country club or other such expenses not really necessary to the business
- Nepotism expenses (salary, autos, computers, vacations, etc.)
- Vacations or other related party travel expenses, including time-share expenses, etc.
- Multiple vehicles or unusual vehicle expenses for the owner, family, etc.
- Excessive insurance to owners and related parties (e.g., life, health, disability)
- Building rent paid by the company to an owner that is in excess of the market value
- Equipment leases paid by the company to an owner that are in excess of the market value
- Professional sports tickets not necessary for the business
- Rental expenses or repairs that would normally be paid by a landlord
- Hobbies such as buying jewelry, antique cars, etc.
- Below-market transfers of assets to related parties or family members
- Discounted sales prices to related parties, friends, etc.
- Costs paid in excess of market to vendors that are related parties or friends
- Discounts or free delivery given to related parties or friends
- Repairs, remodeling, maintenance, insurance or other expenses for a personal residence
- Inventory or scrap sold in cash and not deposited into the company's bank account
- Alimony or child-support payments made by the company

We are not being judgmental about these matters, but it is a fact that some personal expenses occasionally do end up in a company's Income Statement.

There are significant risks associated with being too aggressive on these matters, and it is prudent to discuss these issues with *The Success Team*™. There are important differences between income tax avoidance and income tax evasion.

Income Tax Avoidance – We have certain rights as citizens of the United States to use professionals and knowledge in order to legally avoid paying taxes that are not owed. Below is a definition:

> *Tax avoidance is the legal utilization of the tax regime to one's own advantage to reduce the amount of tax that is payable by means that are within the law.* [86]

Income Tax Evasion – This is significantly different from income tax avoidance:

> *Tax evasion is the general term for efforts by individuals, corporations, trusts and other entities to evade taxes by illegal means. Tax evasion usually entails taxpayers deliberately misrepresenting or concealing the true state of their affairs to the tax authorities to reduce their tax liability and includes in particular dishonest tax reporting, such as declaring less income, profits or gains than actually earned or overstating deductions.* [87]

Amended Tax Returns – You and *The Success Team*™ may decide that it is prudent to amend certain tax returns prior to showing them to the prospective buyer.

Taxes
Checklist

#	Subject	Description	n/a	Assigned To	Expected Completion Date	Completed & in the Data Room
1	Tax Returns	Changes in corporate structure during the past five years				
2	Tax Returns	Copies of all foreign, federal, state and local tax returns for the past three years (e.g., income, franchise, personal property, real estate, sales, use, payroll withholdings)				
3	Tax Notices	Copies of any notices by foreign, federal, state or local authorities regarding taxes owed and/or issues related (e.g., income, franchise, personal property, real estate, sales, use, payroll withholdings)				
4	Unpaid	A list of any unpaid taxes of any kind				
5	NOL, Deferral	A list of net operating loss (NOL) carry forwards and details of any deferred tax liability				
6	Preparers	The name and contact information for the company's tax preparers for the past three years (e.g., income, franchise, personal property, real estate, sales, use, payroll withholdings)				
7	Licenses, Exemptions	Copies of sales and other tax licenses and any tax exemption certificates				
8	Attorney	Copies from attorneys of letters related to taxes, including any appeals or areas of risk to the company				
9	Audits and Settlements	Copies of audits, revenue agent reports, and settlements for the company, including any proposed adjustments by any domestic or foreign government agency, including current ongoing audits				
10	Rulings	Copies of any rulings or concessions that have been obtained from any domestic or foreign government agency				

Taxes
Checklist
(continued)

#	Subject	Description	n/a	Assigned To	Expected Completion Date	Completed & in the Data Room
11	States and Foreign Locations	List of all jurisdictions to which the company pays taxes or should pay taxes, including any government agency, domestic or foreign (e.g., income, franchise, personal property, real estate, sales, use, payroll withholdings)				
12	Challenges	List any actual, anticipated or potential challenges to the company's tax treatment (e.g., income, franchise, personal property, real estate, sales, use, payroll withholdings)				

Chapter 25

Environmental Checklist

Overview – The business community is becoming more sensitive to environmental issues. Much of this is due to recent laws and regulations passed, including many lawsuits filed against businesses for alleged environmental violations.

Your company may or may not have any risk related to this subject, but it is worth your time to study the checklist in this chapter. This subject will be brought to your attention by a prospective buyer.

The environmental rules and regulations are so numerous and comprehensive that they can be overwhelming. **Look at the number of substances** that OSHA's website has listed as hazardous materials:

> *Hazardous and toxic substances are defined as those chemicals present in the workplace which are capable of causing harm. In*

this definition, the term chemicals includes dusts, mixtures, and common materials such as paints, fuels, and solvents. OSHA currently regulates exposure to approximately **400 substances***. The OSHA Chemical Sampling Information file contains listings for approximately* **1,500 substances***; the Environmental Protection Agency's (EPA's) Toxic Substance Control Act (TSCA) Chemical Substances Inventory lists information on more than* **62,000 chemicals** *or chemical substances; some libraries maintain files of material safety data sheets (MSDS) for more than* **100,000 substances**. [88]

Industries – Below is a short list of some of the industries that are affected by environmental laws, rules and regulations. [89]

- **Manufacturing has about 300 subcategories, including**:
  - Dog and cat food manufacturing
  - Soybean processing
  - Breakfast cereal manufacturing
  - Fruit and vegetable canning
  - Ice cream and frozen dessert manufacturing
  - Frozen cakes, pies and other pastries manufacturing
  - Coffee and tea manufacturing
  - Soft drink manufacturing
  - Breweries, wineries and distilleries
  - Digital printing
  - Plastic material manufacturing
  - Pesticide and other agricultural chemical manufacturing
  - Pharmaceutical preparation manufacturing
  - Paint and coating manufacturing
  - Soap and other detergent manufacturing
  - Plastic bottle manufacturing
  - Tire manufacturing
  - Iron, steel, aluminum, copper manufacturing and forging
  - Kitchen utensil, pot and pan manufacturing
  - Machine shops
  - Small arms and ammunition manufacturing
  - Farm machinery and equipment manufacturing
  - Office machinery manufacturing

- Construction has about 25 subcategories, including:
  - Poured concrete foundation and structure contractors
  - Framing and masonry contractors
  - Roofing contractors
  - Electrical contractors
  - Drywall and insulation contractors
  - Carpentry contractors

- Wholesale Trade has about 40 subcategories, including:
  - Stationery and office supplies merchant wholesalers
  - Men's, boys', women's, children's and infants' merchant wholesalers
  - General line and packaged frozen food merchant wholesalers
  - Dairy product merchant wholesalers

- Retail Trade has about 25 subcategories, including:
  - Hardware stores
  - Cosmetic, beauty supplies and perfume stores
  - Pharmacies and drug stores
  - Sporting goods stores
  - Hobby, toy and game stores

- Transportation and Warehousing has about 25 subcategories, including:
  - Passenger and freight air transportation
  - Chartered passenger and air freight transportation
  - Railroads
  - Water freight transportation

- Defense contractors
- Farms
- Oil and gas
- Waste management
- Land development
- Hospitals, health care and social assistance
- Automobile repair shops
- Arts, entertainment and recreation

It may be prudent for you and *The Success Team*™ to consult with an environmental specialist and/or an attorney regarding this subject if you feel your company might be in an industry that is subject to compliance with the environmental checklist in this chapter.

Environmental
Checklist

#	Subject	Description	n/a	Assigned To	Expected Completion Date	Completed & in the Data Room
1	Permits	All environment-related permits issued to and permit applications requested by the company or any subsidiary, and all related memoranda and correspondence				
2	Insurance	All environment-related insurance policies, notices or claims for coverage, responses to any such notices or claims of the company, and any subsidiary or their respective insurance brokers or agents				
3	Agreements	All agreements, consent decrees, orders, judgments or correspondence regarding environmental matters to which the company or subsidiary is a party				
4	Actions or Claims	Document any threatened or pending environmental, litigation, actions or claims in which allegations have been made regarding release or threat of release of hazardous or toxic substances, or regarding injuries to persons or property caused by hazardous or toxic substances				
5	Property	List all real property owned, leased or operated by the company or subsidiaries in the past				
6	Materials	List of all hazardous materials used and/or stored at company or subsidiary, along with a list of hazardous and universal waste generated and disposed of from company activities, including copies of disposal records for the past three years				

Environmental
Checklist
(continued)

#	Subject	Description	n/a	Assigned To	Expected Completion Date	Completed & in the Data Room
7	Liabilities	All documents related to environmental liabilities affecting the company and any subsidiary or their respective operations arising from any acquisition or sale by the company of any asset or business				
8	Reports	All environmental impact reports or statements, including all public notices and comments, prepared in connection with the construction or modification of any facilities belonging to the company or any subsidiary				
9	Attorney	Name, address and contact information of the company's environmental law firm				

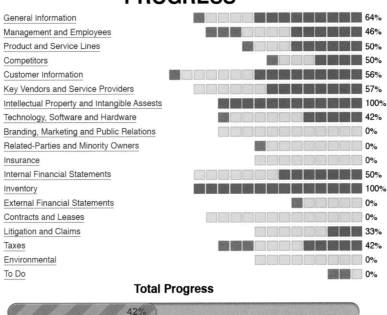

PROGRESS

General Information	64%
Management and Employees	46%
Product and Service Lines	50%
Competitors	50%
Customer Information	56%
Key Vendors and Service Providers	57%
Intellectual Property and Intangible Assests	100%
Technology, Software and Hardware	42%
Branding, Marketing and Public Relations	0%
Related-Parties and Minority Owners	0%
Insurance	0%
Internal Financial Statements	50%
Inventory	100%
External Financial Statements	0%
Contracts and Leases	0%
Litigation and Claims	33%
Taxes	42%
Environmental	0%
To Do	0%

Total Progress

42%

Chapter 26

Tracking the Results
of Your Exit Strategy Process

As you can tell by now, *The Advanced Due Diligence Process*™ is complicated. The preceding chapters have more than 200 tasks to be performed. Some of these might be marked in the future by your company as "not applicable;" however, other such tasks are likely to take their place.

MANAGING THE PROCESS

Either you will manage the exit strategy process or the process will manage you. This is a challenging task, but it can be done with proper management. We have two suggestions that may help you manage the process:

1. Delegate as much as possible to the *Team Manager* of *The Success Team*™.
2. Use our dashboard software to track and manage the process.

TEAM MANAGER

As we discussed in previous chapters, the goal for you as the Finder of the company is to continue increasing revenues and adjusted EBITDA during the exit strategy process. You want to push toward the Desirable and avoid the Undesirable in the following graph:

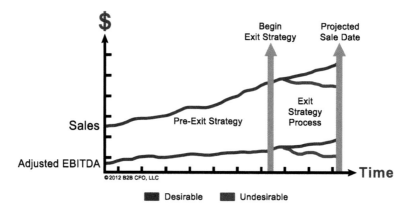

One of the easiest techniques to keep your focus on the Desirable trends on the above chart is to hire a good *Team Manager*. We used the quote below about some of the attributes of the *Team Manager* in a previous chapter.

> *Retain a point person. Even with an inside sale, I believe a third party point person is essential.*
>
> *Rick Rickertsen* [90]

There is no requirement that the *Team Manager* has to be an outside person. There are, however, some advantages of hiring an outside nonemployee as the *Team Manager*. This person:

- Has experience in the exit strategy process
- Is not worried about losing a W-2 job when the transaction closes
- Is focused solely on completing the exit strategy process
- Will help the other team members keep focused on their deadlines
- Can easily and objectively communicate important concerns and issues directly to you
- Allows you to spend less time delegating and following up on matters
- Will give you more time to focus on increasing the value of your business

Below are some suggestions on how to use the *Team Manager* in this process:

- Hire a competent person that has the skills and attributes listed above
- Delegate the details of the process to this person
- Hold a "results" meeting with this person at least once a month
- Adjust priorities, when necessary, and hold the *Team Manager* accountable
- Look at our dashboard software at least once a week to monitor progress

DASHBOARD SOFTWARE

Our dashboard software has been created to let you periodically see the progress of your exit strategy process. It is a great tool for the *Team Manager* to manage the process. The dashboard software contains important information, such as:

- Overall percentage completed on the exit strategy process
- The current value of your company
- Percentage of completion on each individual project
- Anyone who has fewer than 30 days to complete their project
- The name of anyone who is past due on an assignment
- Each document that is stored in your secured Data Room

We highly recommend that you and the *Team Manager* use this high-tech tool to manage the process.

The dashboard demo is at www.b2bexitdemo.com.

There are two ways to obtain a subscription to our dashboard software:

- Through your B2B CFO® partner. You can find the B2B CFO® partner nearest your company's ZIP Code at www.b2bcfo.com.

- Purchase a subscription at www.b2bcfo.com/store.

It is lonely at the top of an organization.

Only the person at the top understands this feeling. Other well-intentioned people may empathize and state that they understand this feeling of loneliness, but they do not.

There was an author who was able to articulate those feelings and give inspirational thought to those at the top of an organization. These words were written more than 100 years ago by James Allen.

We recommend that you read these words any time you get discouraged. You will have many discouraging moments, and these words of wisdom should help inspire you to continue the process toward the ultimate goal of selling your business.

> *The thoughtless, the ignorant, and the indolent, seeing only the apparent effects of things and not the things themselves, talk of luck, of fortune, and chance. Seeing a man grow rich, they say, "How lucky he is!" Observing another become intellectual, they exclaim, "How highly favored he is!" And noting the saintly character and wide influence of another, they remark, "How chance aids him at every turn!"*

> *They do not see the trials and failures and struggles which these men have voluntarily encountered in order to gain their experience. They have no knowledge of the sacrifices they have made, of the undaunted efforts they have put forth, of the faith they have exercised, that they might overcome the apparently insurmountable, and realize the Vision of their heart. They do not know the darkness and the heartaches; they only see the light and*

joy, and call it "luck"; do not see the long and arduous journey but only behold the pleasant goal, and call it "good fortune"; do not understand the process, but only perceive the result and call it "chance."

In all human affairs there are efforts, and there are results, and the strength of the effort is the measure of the result. Chance is not. "Gifts," powers, material, intellectual and spiritual possessions are the fruit of effort. They are thoughts completed, objects accomplished, visions realized. [91]

You now have the tools and the processes to work toward your company's exit strategy process.

We wish you luck and hope that we have added some value to you and your company with the information in this book.

FOOTNOTE REFERENCES

1. Avoiding The Danger Zone, Business Illusions, 28-29.
2. Ibid, 4-5.
3. The Serenity Prayer is the common name for an originally untitled prayer by 20th century American theologian, Reinhold Niebuhr, Wikipedia.
4. The Effective Entrepreneur, 146.
5. The Seven Habits of Highly Effective People, 97.
6. Ibid, 98.
7. Ibid, 101.
8. Avoiding The Danger Zone, Business Illusions, 26.
9. Private Capital Markets, Valuation, Capitalization and Transfer of Private Business Interests, Second Edition, 564-565.
10. Wikipedia, Tsunami.
11. Ibid.
12. www.livescience.com
13. Wikipedia, Tsunami. 24.
14. 11 Things You Absolutely Need To Know About Selling Your Business, 12.
15. Cash Out Move On. Get Top Dollar – And More – Selling Your Business, xv.
16. Finish Big, 68, 77, emphasis added.
17. The Family Business Guide, 161.
18. The Complete Guide to Valuing & Selling Your Business, 5.
19. Avoiding The Danger Zone, Business Illusions, 29.
20. The Complete Guide to Valuing & Selling Your Business, 18.
21. Sell Your Business Your Way, 23
22. Ibid, 99.
23. Cash Out Move On, 100.
24. Ibid, xvii-xviii.
25. Valuing Your Business, 9.
26. Built to Sell, 94.
27. The Complete Guide to Valuing & Selling Your Business, 10.
28. Ibid, 14-27.
29. Private Capital Markets, Valuation, Capitalization and Transfer of Private Business Interests, Second Edition, 49.
30. The Complete Guide to Valuing & Selling Your Business, 14.
31. Manage to Sell Your Business, 89-90.

32. The Complete Guide to Valuing & Selling Your Business, 18.
33. Ibid, 15.
34. Business Exit Planning, 88.
35. Ibid, 88.
36. Ibid, 88.
37. Ibid, 89.
38. 11 Things You Absolutely Need To Know About Selling Your Business, 40.
39. Manage to Sell Your Business, 90.
40. The Complete Guide to Valuing & Selling Your Business, 16.
41. Sell Your Business Your Way, 21.
42. The Complete Guide to Valuing & Selling Your Business, 18.
43. Cash Out Move On, Get Top Dollar – And More – Selling Your Business, 69.
44. Avoiding The Danger Zone, Business Illusions, 26.
45. Sell Your Business Your Way, 3-4, emphasis added.
46. The Danger Zone, Lost in the Growth Transition, 18-39.
47. Ibid, 26.
48. Avoiding The Danger Zone, Business Illusions, 6.
49. Cash Out Move On, Get Top Dollar – And More – Selling Your Business, 163.
50. Built to Sell, 127-128.
51. Cash Out Move On, Get Top Dollar – And More – Selling Your Business, 74-75, emphasis added.
52. Valuing Your Business, Strategies to Maximize the Sale Price, 24.
53. Private Capital Markets, Valuation, Capitalization, and Transfer of Private Business Interests, Second Edition, 563.
54. Exit Strategy: Maximizing The Value Of Your Business, Third Edition, 13.
55. Manage to Sell Your Business, xviii.
56. Valuing Your Business, Strategies To Maximize The Sales Price, 61.
57. 11 Things You Absolutely Need To Know About Selling Your Business, 21.
58. Business Exit Planning, 6-7.
59. Cash Out Move On, Get Top Dollar – And More – Selling Your Business, 161.
60. Cash Out Move On, Get Top Dollar – And More – Selling Your Business, 194.
61. Valuing Your Business, Strategies to Maximize the Sales Price, 63
62. Business Exit Planning, 138.
63. Sell Your Business Your Way, 148-149.
64. Business Exit Planning, 138, emphasis added.

65. Ibid, 139.
66. Ibid, 139.
67. Wikipedia, Virtual Data Room.
68. Business Exit Planning, 138.
69. Manage to Sell Your Business, 90.
70. Valuing Your Business, Strategies to Maximize the Sales Price, 28.
71. Delivering Happiness, A Path to Profits Passion and Purpose, 121, emphasis added.
72. The Family Business Guide, 104.
73. Built to Sell, 94.
74. Wikipedia, Joe Robbie.
75. www.forbes.com/2006/12/04/estate-tax-estee-lauder-irs-ent-law-cx_mf_1204estatetax.html.
76. www.findmyinsurance.com/financialplanningarticle.htm, emphasis added.
77. The Kiplinger Magazine, Changing Times, January 1986, 66.
78. Avoiding The Danger Zone, Business Illusions, 107.
79. Cash Out Move On, Get Top Dollar – And More – Selling Your Business, 99-100.
80. Ibid, 101.
81. Valuing Your Business, Strategies to Maximize the Sales Price, 33.

82. Cash Out Move On, Get Top Dollar – And More – Selling Your Business, 99.
83. Ibid, 166, emphasis added.
84. Wikipedia, Opinion
85. The Complete Guide to Valuing & Selling Your Business, 15.
86. Wikipedia, tax avoidance.
87. Wikipedia, tax evasion.
88. http://www.osha.gov/SLTC/hazardoustoxicsubstances/index.html
89. See some of this information in: 2011 Oklahoma Most Hazardous Industry per North American Industry Classification System (NAICS) Codes, January 12, 2011 (This report is a state report using Bureau of Labor Statistics (BLS) published data.
90. Sell Your Business Your Way, 23
91. As A Man Thinketh, 56-57.

Acknowledgement

Curt Sahakian's
Due Diligence Checklists
Questions to Ask Before You Buy or
Partner with a Company

Index